WALTER A. TEAL

HANDBOOK
of
SCHOOL LETTERS

HANDBOOK
of
SCHOOL LETTERS

Knute Larson
James H. McGoldrick

Parker Publishing Company, Inc.

West Nyack, N. Y.

© 1970, BY
PARKER PUBLISHING COMPANY, INC
WEST NYACK, NEW YORK

Fifth Printing.....March, 1972

LIBRARY OF CONGRESS
CATALOG CARD NUMBER: 71-102199

PRINTED IN THE UNITED STATES OF AMERICA
B & P—0-13-381285-5

Dedicated to

Ruth Larson and Terry McGoldrick

Other Books by Knute Larson

Effective Secondary School Discipline

Guide to Personal Advancement

in the Teaching Profession

A Word from the Authors
About Using This Book

Education is an extremely demanding profession. Teachers, counselors, specialists, and administrators know that to survive they must communicate—and they must communicate well. While one-to-one communication may be the quickest and most popular way to transmit information, ideas, and orders, it is certainly not the only effective way. Carefully written correspondence also gets things done *and* it provides a record for reference.

Each day brings a complete set of new problems, many of which appear in the daily torrent of incoming mail. Unless you give this correspondence your best efforts, the result will reflect negatively and directly on your professional competence. If correspondence is treated as a nuisance to be disposed of quickly, new problems of greater dimensions may be generated. The new problems will probably be more time consuming than the old ones. Time is important to you. *Good correspondence saves time.*

This book is a manual of educational correspondence and a broad collection of effective samples that will provide you with short-cuts for your daily tasks. All samples are related to realistic problems faced daily in American schools. They relate to the best current practices. In one chapter dealing with the paperwork of professional negotiations we cover a problem area that is relatively new to the American scene. The establishment of ground rules and procedures, the reporting of progress to teachers, minutes of meetings, mediation correspondence, and excerpts from a contract are included to help you with this rapidly growing process which involves teachers, administrators, and school boards.

All forms of written communications required of educators are covered in the form of actual model letters and memos dealing with all phases of school operations. The entire hiring and firing cycles are arranged in sequences by sample letters. Teachers' letters to parents are represented by samples in a wide variety of subject areas. The discipline and guidance functions are heavily represented in model correspondence. All these samples can be used as patterns or as models by you or by your secretary. You will also find useful hints on the efficient use of telegrams, printed cards, postcards, letters, and memos.

The simple index will enable you to find quickly sample letters on personal matters, business operations, curriculum development, community obligations of educators, student affairs, home-school communications, and even your own career advancement.

In addition to the large variety of effective letters, you will also find practical guidance in writing regulations, policies, and job descriptions. While these cannot be strictly classified as correspondence, they do represent common writing tasks faced by all administrators and some teachers from time to time.

The words "model" and "pattern" are used in this book frequently. They refer to types of letters which you can use as samples for your own correspondence. The words are used to define letters printed here with the intent that you will, or can, use these in your own situation. Hence, as you will note while reading, we omit school and personal names from all letters, making it easier for your secretary to insert your school name and whatever personal names might be in order.

Model and pattern letters are not necessarily form letters although they can be. In our view many of the letters we print will be typed individually by your secretary and sent to a single person. Such individual typing does not destroy their model or pattern classification. Other letters, however, will be duplicated in one way or another for a large distribution as is usually done with form letters; these, too, can be written from the patterns we offer in subsequent chapters.

All sample letters reflect sound practices. Whenever possible, they are arranged in a sequence that simulates actual procedures.

Keep this book near your desk. It will help you, and your secretary, produce written correspondence that will represent *the real you*.

Knute Larson

James H. McGoldrick

Table of Contents

HANDBOOK
of
SCHOOL LETTERS

ONE

Your Correspondence

Is You

Dear Mrs. _____:

Your son, _____, was referred to my office yesterday for violation of our Student Code of Behavior. I feel that it is necessary at this time to call your attention to his serious attitudinal deficiencies in respect to his peer relationships.

This matter reflects his general level of frustration and apathy toward curricular matters as well. No doubt he considers this an insoluable problem due to his verbal deficiencies in relation to his track level assignment. I can assure you that his aptitude profile shows otherwise.

I would appreciate your discussing this matter with him immediately.

Yours Very Truly,

You don't believe this letter is real? Neither did we at first. Unfortunately, it is a nearly verbatim reproduction of a letter actually sent by a school administrator to a parent with a sixth grade education. It could have been worse: it could have gone to a parent with a college education.

What in heaven's name did the boy do? Was it serious? What "matter" should be discussed with him? What does all the pompous gobbledegook mean? Even if this letter were to be translated from pedagese to English, it would say very little. We do not contend that this sample is typical of all school correspondence, but we know that too often letters nearly as bad as this represent the school to the community. Most of the time this results from hasty and careless handling of daily correspondence.

Do you hurry your correspondence to get it out of the way? Do you check it over before you sign it? An experienced journalist can crank out acceptable first draft material to meet deadlines. He has to do this at any hour of the night or day—fresh or tired. You may not possess this gift. Why try to duplicate the journalist's first draft skill? Unlike the working newsman, you are not usually tied to absolutely rigid daily deadlines. Nothing forces you to delay your correspondence until you are deep in the valley of afternoon fatigue. You can accent the positive and regard your correspondence as an opportunity to express your views. You can view it as a way to get things done quickly. You can put your best image forward.

DECISIONS, DECISIONS

Testing Your Letters

A great deal of damage can be done by poorly written letters which may turn up later to haunt you. Realization of the harmful use to which your poor prose can be put should lead to your first rule: Never let any written communication leave your desk unless it says precisely what you want it to say with as much skill as you can muster.

This decision has binding implications. Initially, it means that you will rarely send out a first draft of anything but the most routine replies or queries. Instead, you will reread what you have written and apply to it some simple tests:

- Is this letter necessary in the first place? If not, how can I better communicate?
- Is this letter devoted to a single topic? If not, have I made it crystal clear where I shift gears from one topic to another?
- Have I broken down into shorter sentences those long, involved statements which confuse me when I read them?
- Have I made the letter as brief as possible without losing clarity?
- Have I used a personal touch where it should be used?

If the Assistant Principal who wrote our opening letter had taken time to apply these tests, he might have written something else:

Dear Mrs. _____:

Your son, _____, was sent to me for breaking school rules yesterday. He left a classroom without permission. This is serious. However, I was more disturbed by his resentful attitude when I talked with him.

He does not seem to be getting along well with other students in his class. I think his real problem is that he believes his work is too hard for him.

I explained to him that his past record and his test scores prove that he is able to do this work. I am afraid that he did not believe me.

At this time I think he needs encouragement more than he needs punishment. I hope we can work together to help him. Why don't you call and make an appointment to talk with his counselor, Miss _____. Show her this letter when you see her.

If you want more information from me, please call _____ _____ and ask for me.

Very truly yours,

The Time for Writing

One of the secrets of good communications is to select a time or times during the day when you can work without interruption. This is difficult for most administrators, but it is not impossible. You do not need a *long* period of time. If you get to work immediately, you will be amazed at what can be accomplished in 15–20 minutes. Some people find it convenient to put off writing tasks until students and staff have left the building for the day. Others prefer to get at them as soon as the morning's amenities and rituals are finished. We believe that two brief periods reserved each day offer distinct advantages.

There is something to say for sorting correspondence into two categories—routine responses and those requiring some thought. Thus, the routine letters can be handled early and the more difficult ones at a later time. This procedure allows you to take advantage of peripheral thinking during odd moments of a busy day before tackling important correspondence. The value of a decision at four in the afternoon is perceptibly increased after the problem has been exposed to a full day of seemingly imperceptible consideration.

Having established optimum times for letter writing, stick to your schedule except in emergencies. You may want to block the time out on your daily calendar so that your secretary can protect you from minor interruptions. Be certain that she knows that you view correspondence as an important part of your work and that you intend to do it right.

A wise approach might be to set aside two separate writing periods each day as suggested above. Do the routine in the morning; start difficult letters at the later time, holding rewriting until the following day. You may wish to have your secretary do some preliminary sorting before you divide the letters into the two suggested major categories. If all incoming correspondence is separated into general categories before it is given to you, your effectiveness might improve because you can concentrate on one type of problem at a time.

Put It on the Record

Educational administration sometimes seems to survive on a diet of red tape and memoranda liberally sprinkled with a condiment of buck passing. Some use this as an excuse to avoid the written forms of communication. "Why add to the paperwork?" they ask. The effective administrator knows this can be an oversimplification. There is a time to write and there is a time not to write. The effective man knows when to get his views on record.

A principal may ask his superior several times by telephone to have a set of stairs repaired. His superior may forget or may delay action. A student may break a leg. How can the principal prove that no actionable negligence was involved?

Had he written a letter or memo to his superior, pointing out the potential danger and requesting a high priority for the repair work, his carbon copy of the request could save the day, at least for him. Had he written a second request after receiving no action on the first one, it would have become forcefully clear to his superior that *the responsibility had now shifted up the line,* and that this was on record. The stairs would have been repaired and a student would have been spared an injury.

Correspondence of this type can have unpleasant implications. It should be carefully and politely worded. This helps prevent petty vendettas from developing. Being polite, however, does not require that the administrator become a paper tiger: You *can* be both polite and firm. Consider the following:

MEMORANDUM

To: Dr. _____, Superintendent of Schools
From: Mr. _____, Swimming Pool Supervisor
Date: June 17, 19__
Subject: Unsafe Conditions at High School Pool

For six weeks we have been trying to get the Maintenance Department to fill in the holes in the tile caused by the removal of the diving tower. These holes are only ⅜ inches deep and about 2 inches in diameter but they can cause a running student to trip and fall.

I, hereby, officially declare the pool unsafe for student use until the repairs are completed. The responsibility is now yours.

MEMORANDUM

To: Mr. _____, Swimming Pool Supervisor
From: Dr. _____, Superintendent of Schools
Date: June 19, 19__
Subject: Unsafe Conditions at High School Pool

It was my understanding that the repairs you refer to in your memo were to have been made between the close of the regular school year and the opening of your summer program. In the meantime, you were to exercise extra caution in the area. The specific danger you mention (running) is prohibited in the pool area. Have your teachers enforced this rule?

Unfortunately, other pressing safety matters in the District require a high priority in the use of our maintenance men. The pool tile cannot be repaired until the end of August.

Since you are our expert on pool safety, I shall be guided by your recommendation. I shall prepare a directive (citing your advice) that the pool is to be closed until repairs are completed. This will, of course, eliminate the summer program for which you receive extra compensation. I will try to assign to other duties all members of the physical education department who were scheduled to work in the pool area this summer.

MEMORANDUM

To: Dr. _____, Superintendent of Schools
From: Mr. _____, Swimming Pool Supervisor
Date: June 20, 19__
Subject: Temporary Condition of Tile at High School Pool

I have conferred with my colleagues and we have decided that careful supervision of the area in question will eliminate the problem until repairs are made.

We certainly hope that repairs can be made as soon as possible. It would be a shame to deny the safety and recreational values of the pool to our children in the summer.

With our extra precautions the pool will be safe. Please disregard my memo of June 17.

A superintendent may see his Board as a group once or twice a month. He can save valuable time if he prepares them for the formal sessions by sending to the members, periodically between meetings, memos outlining the pros and cons of impending action and his recommendations. Copies of some of these memos can be used as is or adapted to be used as press handouts.

One of the more common criticisms of superintendents by School Boards is lack of sufficient information given by the administration to the Board. Frequent letters or memos delivered between meetings are better from an informational viewpoint than the same quantity of material issued as a massive distribution just before meeting time. A memo covering one point will get undivided attention if delivered by itself in the quiet time of an "off week." The same memo will attract scant attention if delivered in a mass of material just before meeting night.

Administrators, teachers, and other school employees can and usually do get better and faster action when requests are put in writing. A complicated matter outlined carefully in a letter can be read and reread for better understanding. It also carries the weight of being on record, especially if a distribution of copies is indicated in the usual manner.

The examples used above do not needlessly multiply paperwork. They serve, instead, to get vital matters on paper and into the hands of those who need to know about them. This, perhaps above all, is the best test when facing a decision whether to write or not to write: Is this important enough to bring forcefully to someone's attention? If not, you may rely on oral communication and the memory of your clients and colleagues; but, if it is really important, get it on paper, on record, and out to those who need to know.

And keep the carbon.

CHOOSING A FORM OF CORRESPONDENCE

Written communications may take any form, from love letters in the sand to inspirational words on a bronze plaque. Each form has its own advantages and disadvantages. Consider these before adopting a particular approach. Does the form chosen offer the best chance for effectively communicating what I want to say?

The following is a brief survey of the more common forms of written communication used in school operations. Each form is covered in more detail later in the book along with appropriate examples.

The Standard Personal Letter

This is the most appropriate form of communication when some sort of social bond exists between the writer and the reader. It is useful also when there are no such bonds. It has a wide range of school applications.

The standard letter can carry a personal touch lacking in most other written forms. Often this touch can help cut red tape and expedite action. A friendly letter asking for prompt delivery is better than a brusque demand, especially when action must be carried out at a low level. Management wants to retain even a grouchy customer but the clerk who reads your letter, the man who must initiate the necessary action, does not necessarily care enough about you to overlook an insult, real or imagined. This is where the personal touch, the bit of humanity, may pay off for you.

One caution is in order. If you decide to write a personal letter, *make it personal*. Get into it some reference that shows it is not a form letter. Refer to the specific event or person or thing that prompts you to write, and do it as early in the letter as possible.

The disadvantages of the personal letter lie chiefly in that each must be individually composed if it is to contain the required specific references. Obviously, this forces you to devote more time to writing than does the use of a form letter. The use of a pattern letter often represents a suitable compromise which enables you to avoid the obvious form letter while saving most of the writing time that a personal letter requires.

The Memorandum

The most common form of internal communication, the ubiquitous memo, can be a significant time saver with its TO, FROM, SUBJECT, DATE format. It can be made more effective by inserting routing information as part of the printed head, especially in those districts or schools where standard distribution lists have been compiled. The memo can provide for multiple distribution easily and effectively. Usually, but not always, memos are brief.

The disadvantages of the memo are many. They often become absurd, like those often widely distributed ones calling for intense efforts to save paper. Some of the memos in *Up the Down Staircase* could serve as educational classics. Other disadvantages of the memo lie in their impersonality, in their multiplicity, in their very ordinariness. Often administrators compound the faults of the memo by making them overly long or by crowding a diversity of topics helter-skelter into the same missive.

Of all written school communications, the memo should be subjected to rigorous examination before the administrator starts to write:

- Is this memo really necessary? Could I talk to someone rather than send this out? Will the phone serve as well or better?
- Will the memo be read by the person or persons for whom it is intended?
- If the subject is that important, how and when will I follow it up?
- If a meeting will be necessary anyhow, should I call the meeting first, explain the subject, and then hand out copies of the memo for the record?

The administrator who decides to write a memo should spend a reasonable amount of time on it in order to avoid the impression of an imperial command or plain bad manners. There is no reason for the complete omission of words such as "please" and "thank you" from memos, yet these words are rarely included despite the fact that they do no harm to the message. Nor is there any excuse for brusqueness.

Daily every administrator and teacher faces an avalanche of printed and duplicated materials. Each reacts in a perfectly human manner. Telegrams get read first. Then come the personal letters, card, and memos. Duplicated materials are read last, if at all.

The Postcard

The postcard is a neglected means of communications in most schools. It is easy to use, convenient, and economical. It requires only that the message be brief and non-confidential. As an enclosure in a letter asking for a response, a self-addressed stamped postcard is almost a guarantee of a swift reply. The wise school district makes available a supply of postcards to encourage the saving of time and money.

A few suggested uses of postcards would be:

- To remind people about meetings.
- To acknowledge receipt of materials.
- To request or to supply routine information.
- To acknowledge receipt of important documents such as college transcripts.

The Form Letter

Few devices save as much administrative effort as the form letter which is specifically prepared to be used in a large number of related cases. Time is saved in highly repetitive correspondence such as routine notices to parents. Necessary lengthy excerpts from policies or regulations can be distributed in this manner. Once prepared properly, the good form letter can serve almost indefinitely.

These require special care, however, since few things can cause as much trouble as a misdirected or ill-conceived form letter. They should be avoided in truly important matters, *especially when the news is bad*. No parent wants to learn by a form letter that Junior will not graduate with his class. No parent wants to learn by form letter that Suzy must be dropped by the choir because her conduct is more chorus than choir. Bad news should be transmitted in person at a conference, if possible, or by phone, if need be, and followed by an individual confirming letter.

Good news can be sent by a form letter. It is appropriate to send such a letter to every member of the senior play telling each one how much you enjoyed the production. Degree is also important: A form letter would not be appropriate for the teacher who directed the play.

The time saving qualities of this device are frequently offset by the impersonality of such letters, by their obvious nature which leads some to believe they are afterthoughts, and by the poor runoff jobs often done on them. These disadvantages should be weighed by the administrator in advance, and the finished product should be carefully checked before it is sent out.

The Pattern Letter

The pattern letter differs from the form letter in the same manner that the dress a housewife makes from a pattern differs from the dress sold off the rack. There is a margin for individuality within the pattern which is constructed to serve a number of individual cases rather than to blanket a whole category of cases.

A file of these letters should be prepared to assist your secretary in those routine matters that require more than a form letter but which can be handled with less than a personal note. The annual request for a clergyman to offer benediction at graduation is an example. Two or three patterns should be available, however, so that one clergyman does not receive the same letter time after time. There are numerous periodic events that can be served by such letters. The effort of individual composition seems a waste in these cases.

Pattern letters have disadvantages as do all types of letters. They may seem too impersonal to some potential writers. Unless care is taken, two or more people who thought they got individual letters might discover that they received copies of the same letter. Impersonality is almost inevitable.

Duplicated Letters

These differ from form letters in that they are usually one-time affairs. They should be avoided if possible. They can be used when a large number of people must be notified of an important matter. The sender can add a personal touch to these by signing each and by having the address and salutation typed individually.

The best way to reproduce mass letters or memos is to use a tape activated typewriter which can type the same material over and over at incredible speed. Then, using the same machine—or one with similar type—the letters can be individually addressed and signed so that each appears to be a personal letter. Letters done this way are common in sales operations and in political campaigns but they are uncommon in school districts. They may have value in large operations but their use in small schools is marginal at best since their justification lies almost exclusively in quantity production.

Commercial Greeting Cards

Commercial greeting cards are another of those often overlooked means of communication, except at Christmas. An administrator with a small staff can create much goodwill by sending birthday cards to his people at the proper time each year. He can also send other commercial cards on appropriate occasions such as the birth of a child or the receipt of a masters degree. A stockpile of these can be built with scant trouble. This will negate the need for hurried shopping trips.

Common caution must be exercised in this. Know the people to whom you will send the cards. Don't send stuffy Miss Jones one of those far out cards that fractured the boys at the Elks. Be careful also that you not show undue favoritism in the use of such cards. People expect that you will send these to your personal friends and they will not question their non-inclusion in this group, but if you send cards to *some* staff members, you must be sure to send them to all equivalent staffers at the proper time.

Telegrams

Telegrams are less expensive than commonly supposed, especially if sent to locations within 125 miles. They always get prompt attention and they indicate more than ordinary thoughtfulness on the part of the sender. A *Fast Telegram* takes precedence over all traffic at any time and is delivered immediately (or relayed by phone and delivered later). A *Day Letter* may be deferred but will reach its destination within an hour. A *Night Letter* is the most economical telegram and it will be accepted until 2 A.M. for delivery the following morning. Western Union provides a wide variety of model telegrams.

When placing orders for telegrams, be certain to specify that you want the telegram delivered, not phoned. If you want a copy for your files, you must state this also when placing your order. An almost superfluous caution is not to send telegrams to families with sons serving in the armed forces.

YOU AND YOUR SECRETARY

The administrator who is served by a private secretary learns quickly how important she is to his success and how easily she can contribute to his failure. She must be loyal and discreet as well as professionally competent. The administrator must set the proper tone as soon as the relationship begins. He must make clear exactly what is expected of the secretary. It is his responsibility to see that she is protected from an unreasonable work load, from abusive behavior from angry callers, and that she progresses on the salary schedule as she should.

A good secretary can create an atmosphere that is pleasant even on Monday morning. A bad secretary can create an atmosphere of perpetual, grinding agony. Everyone has faults, of course, and many can be overlooked in the case of a normally productive person. Some secretarial shortcomings can be corrected. Others are intolerable.

If your secretary makes typing errors or errors in transcribing, she deserves an opportunity to sharpen her professional tools. If she cannot do this in a reasonable time, she must be transferred to a less critical position or dismissed. The same would be true of carelessness in dress, appearance, or manners.

If, however, she is guilty of any one of the following, either she or you must go:

- Gossip about what goes on in the office.
- A persistent tendency to move into administrative decision making. Constant efforts to influence your decisions.
- A persistently negative and cheerless attitude.

Each of the above is a cardinal sin which cannot be tolerated. Civil service, tenure laws, union problems notwithstanding, the transgressor *must go*. Life is too short for the administrator to tolerate such problems. He already has one of the most difficult jobs in modern society.

You and your secretary can establish a plan for handling correspondence which will save both of you the most time. You can produce a product in which you can both take pride. The chapters following will show you how to combine all the appropriate forms of correspondence in the way most effective for you.

YOUR FILES

Your secretary should maintain files of all but your most personal correspondence. If she is competent, she will be able to dig out the letter you suddenly need in the middle of a telephone conversation and have it in your hand in a minute or so. Remember, though, too many emergency requests and she may not be able to finish those letters on her desk.

It is worth your while to take time to learn *her* filing system. She may be on vacation when you need to find something. It would be foolish to have to wait until her return because you had not taken the time to learn how to locate things.

You probably want to maintain a personal correspondence file in your desk, at home, or in both places. Perhaps you are an officer of a club or lodge. Maybe your college alumni association corresponds with you frequently. You may carry on continuing, sporadic correspondence with distant friends or relatives. All of this material can be filed and indexed for ready reference *if you take the time to do it properly*. You may use words or phrases like the following for indexing purposes: *Parents, Teachers, Rotary, Harvard—Placement, Harvard School of Ed., Smith—Uncle Harry, Birthdays,* etc.

Common sense should dictate the labels, but more than one administrator has "lost" an important letter because he forgot his own classification clue or because he filed it hastily. Suppose, for example, you receive a letter from one of your former students, a teacher in your school, a Harvard alumnus, etc. The letter is a request that you write a reference supporting his son's application to Harvard. Instead of using the subject matter as a clue and filing it properly, you slip it hastily into one of the Harvard folders (none of which has to do with *student* placement or admission). You just might fail to find it if you look for it after a few weeks. File it under its major topic and, if you are extra cautious, develop a suitable cross index system.

SOME BASIC RULES FOR GOOD CORRESPONDENCE

Use Good Stationery

Many districts practice a relentless economy, a false economy, by using cheap paper for letters and by having this imprinted in the high school shop. Use your influence to change this procedure. The paper on which the letter is written says something about you and your school before a word has been read. Have your district buy good paper for ordinary correspondence and have them buy the best available bond for special letters. Use your own money if the school board won't spend theirs. Have the letterhead printed professionally. The cost is less than you think it is. The difference between good printing on good paper and amateur printing on poor paper represents one of those small things that distinguishes the desirable from the routine. Your paper, and the envelopes in which you mail your letters, say a great deal about you. Let them speak favorably.

Similiar comments can be made about the paper you use for memos and other duplicated notices. These need not be the best quality available, but they should never be the poorest either.

Send Only Clean Copy

Read everything before it is sent out from your office. The best secretary makes errors that she misses in her proofreading. Once the item goes out the error becomes yours, not hers. This is so whether you have read it or not. Impress upon your secretary that no written communication can leave your office until you have read it. Your perusal will catch errors; your approval will free your secretary from responsibility and place the blame for *any error* where it belongs—on you.

Do not permit material to go out if it contains too many erasures, even if they are well-corrected. Set a limit on these and be sure that your secretary knows what that limit is. Encourage her to use one of the correcting tapes when possible. Do not tolerate smudges and forbid creases where no creases are supposed to be.

Establish the rules on this early and stick to them. Typing ability will increase dramatically when the typist must redo sloppy letters.

Remember to be nice about these things. You need not harp or hector to make your point. Just be firm and consistent.

Use Familiar Formats

The

odd

format

has

a

place

in things
but it is not in letter writing. Unless there is a good and specific reason for using avant-garde format, stick to the conventional. Imaginative and arty letter forms are attractive, so attractive that they frequently draw attention away from the content. Unless they reinforce content, the unusual arrangements should be left in the style books.

This does not mean that your letter should flit verbally from cliché to cliché. Your wording should be as original as you can make it, providing that you remain within the limits established by the need for others to understand what you are saying. Your purpose is to communicate, not to show off.

Use Language Appropriate for the Reader

As is true in many professions, we educators have developed our own language. Full of pretentious, polysyllabic clichés, it is often called *pedagese* or *educationese*. The opening letter in this chapter is a pungent example of pedagese. It is a patois that confuses most people including those who use it. It impresses few. It fills our learned colleagues in other disciplines with contempt.

However, constant exposure to some of these clichés causes them to slip into our vocabularies. We do fall into the habit of using them. This can be acceptable when educators speak to other educators. Within the family the clichés can serve as a sort of communications shorthand.

These phrases may not mean the same thing to parents, however, and they may mean even less to that young unmarried reporter who covers the schools for the local paper. The same word is open to a variety of interpretations as, for example, an "experimental" program can mean one thing to a teacher, another to a college graduate parent, something entirely different to a parent who did not finish elementary school. It is your job to make certain that the wording you use is appropriate to the audience for whom you are writing. The same responsibility would hold for the format of the letter and for things like suitable sentence length.

Don't Strut When You Write

Often something seems to happen to people when they sit down to write. The man who is marvelously expressive in speech becomes confusing in his writing. The man who is never misunderstood when he speaks becomes chaotic when he picks up a pen. The explanation is usually simple. The man who is expressive and easily understood is that way because he sticks to ordinary words in his speech. He becomes confusing and chaotic in his writing because, for some reason, he thinks he must reach for polysyllabics. It was Winston Churchill, no mean writer, who said that short words are better than long words, and old words best of all.

Your letters need not be literary masterpieces. They need not be stylistic models. But they must communicate, they must be clear. If you habitually use a rich, extensive vocabulary, use it in letters to learned people so long as you are writing naturally. But avoid this when writing to parents whom you know to be less fortunate educationally than yourself. This does not mean that you have to write down to people. A simple letter with direct words and a preponderance of declarative sentences will not offend an educated man and it will be easily understood by those less well educated. Write as you speak, simply and to be understood. Never write down: It's an insult.

Don't Forget Common Sense

Letters written in anger should be set aside to cool off for at least a day, maybe more. Once that metal lid closes on the mailbox, it is too late to reconsider. Some administrators react to a dictating machine and become ravenous tigers intent upon chewing up the world. Balance, judgment, the attributes we get paid for seem to disappear from some administrative heads the moment they set out to put words on paper. Never write anything to anyone unless you are willing to say it to his face. Perhaps we can go further and state that there are many things you can say to a person that you should not write to him. Angry spoken words will usually fade with time. Angry written words are always there, ready to be exhumed and reread to raise their anger again.

Be careful also with humor when you write. Do not poke fun at anyone in your writing. Leave the insult gags to the night club comics. Remember also the old adage to refrain from speaking about rope to the family of a man who has been hanged.

Do Unto Others . . .

The Golden Rule, which is really the foundation of courtesy in our society, applies to correspondence. Are you pleased when a business letter from someone you know slightly asks you to do something? How about a brief reference to some amusing experience shared by the writer and the reader? A query about your golf handicap? Do you enjoy having weeks pass without an answer to that letter you sent? Do you welcome the impolite phrase?

Do unto others. . . .

"You" Beats "I"

People are perverse. They usually are more interested in their own lives than in yours. They react better to a letter that dwells on "you," the recipient, rather than on "I," the writer. The "you" letter will get more attention on the receiving end and there will still be room in it for the message—even for some personal news from your end.

Use a Writing Method That Makes You Comfortable

The pool players say that you should always shoot your best stick. So it is with the technique of writing letters. Some executives can dictate as well as they can write. Others can turn out better material with a pencil. Some find that they work best on a typewriter. Find your best stick and develop it. Use it for all non-routine items in your correspondence.

Routine work should be handled by dictation if possible. This technique does save time. With modern equipment you can do your dictation anywhere, even while driving your car. Remember, though, that dictated letters are seldom rewritten unless the typist does a poor job of transcription. Handwritten letters are often revised *even by those who never redo dictated material.* You should make it a point to go carefully over letters transcribed from your dictation. You are a rare individual if you cannot improve your material significantly by writing it over and revising it at least once.

A good secretary with a supply of pattern letters can cut dictation time to a minimum. The administrator may say, for example, "Give this one the polite no." Most secretaries can take it from there. Perhaps, in some cases, a pattern letter might be needed as a guide. In any event, the administrator's involvement is cut to a few seconds. This is the important thing.

Memos to staff members outlining a recommended procedure in curriculum change or in budget preparation should usually be handwritten or typed and rewritten to avoid repetition and ambiguity. When you dictate a fairly lengthy memo, it is difficult to avoid repeating the vital points. Some of this is necessary for emphasis or review but it should be limited. Random and rambling repetition is deadly.

Some executives who detest writing have most of their correspondence handled by a subordinate. This may be necessary for very important people with widespread responsibilities, but it is hardly appropriate for the educational administrator who is supposed to be articulate—whose job depends upon his ability to communicate.

An educational administrator cannot escape some personal involvement in correspondence. Cut corners as much as you can by dictation, form letters, pattern letters, etc., but do find the most comfortable modus operandi for you in writing the letters *you* must write. Then rewrite them at least once to make certain that they represent you in the way you want to be represented.

TWO

Use Correspondence
to Ease the Recruiting Job

A SCHOOL IS PEOPLE

A school district consists of many things: buildings, buses, projectors, and lesson plans. It is hardware, software, and money. But mostly it is *people* acting with and in relation to each other. A skilled teacher can perform her daily major and minor miracles despite poor environment and with minimal equipment—if she has to. She can overcome the handicaps of poor administration and weak planning. On the other hand, incompetent teachers will accomplish next to nothing in spite of the best curriculum guides and texts, extensive and expensive hardware, and a modern building.

This is also true of administrators, specialists, and the myriad non-professionals who support the important central business that goes on in the classroom between student and teacher. Since people are central to the process of education, it follows that the administrator's single most important job must be in the area of personnel—recruitment, training, and retention of good people. When the superintendent and his board fight for an adequate budget they are fighting for a better staff. Supervision and in-service education exist solely for the purpose of upgrading classroom experiences. Every line administrator should be, primarily, an instructional leader. We simply cannot overstate the importance of people—good people—in education.

Almost any American educator would offer strong verbal support for this position. But seldom does that educator practice in personnel procedures what he preaches in his philosophy. As a matter of fact, observations of his procedures lead to the conclusion that this area is the *least* important of all.

Large urban districts that are crying for teachers often strangle applicants with red tape. Many suburban districts, conscious of their alleged advantages, behave as though candidates should be rushing to their doors. Rural districts often resign themselves to hiring unqualified local candidates on the assumption that no outsiders could possibly be attracted to their poorly supported schools. Tradition, smugness, lack of money, whatever the reasons for the behavior, American schools in general are not attracting their share of superior people into their classrooms.

This should make administrators eager to do all they can to get the best people possible. This chapter is concerned with one phase of personnel administration—a phase in which a significant number of poor practices predominate. Badly written letters, unnecessary delays in replies, and a generally cavalier attitude toward applicants do cause the loss of many good candidates who turn their attention to other districts that seem to care enough about people to prove it in their practices.

Candidates often have little on which to judge a school district in the early stages of inquiry and application. The district's general reputation may be known, things like the location and proximity of graduate schools may have their influence, salary is always important; but in the early stages the candidate must judge the district by its correspondence. Delay, carelessness, vagueness, uncertainty result in "no sale" as far as a good applicant is concerned. Strict observance of a few simple rules can go a long way toward encouraging good people to sign on the dotted line:

- Every letter of application should be answered promptly even if circumstances limit the reply to a mere acknowledgment and a promise of further correspondence later. A phone call also deserves prompt written verification of what was said in response to the query.
- All letters from applicants should be answered as truthfully as courtesy permits. If there is no appropriate vacancy, say so.
- Send individually dictated letters if possible. If this cannot be done, use individually typed pattern letters. Use mass produced form letters only as a last resort or for special circumstances.
- Strive for the personal touch and show that you are interested in the applicant as a person.
- Keep replies brief and specific but do not hesitate to send supporting items such as recruiting brochures.

- Use good paper and put your best typist on this job.
- Don't be afraid to sell your good points and be frank about your outstanding problems.

REPLIES TO THE FIRST LETTER FROM AN APPLICANT

Administration to Candidate:

Reply to the candidate's letter when information is incomplete.

There are times when you must answer a query even though you do not have all the information you would like to have. The only thing to do in such circumstances is to answer promptly and make an attempt to keep communications open between you. If possible, offer an alternative or a date by which the information will be available.

Dear Mr. _____:

Thank you for your letter inquiring about a teaching position at the sixth grade level. At the moment we anticipate a retirement at the primary level but we know of no possible vacancy which might develop at the sixth grade level. It would be helpful to me to know if you would be interested in teaching at any other grade than the one you indicated in your query.

Enclosed is a brochure describing our district and our surrounding cultural and recreational facilities. Enclosed also is an application form which you might like to submit.

Sincerely,

Administration to Candidate:

*Reply to a candidate when there are
no vacancies in his area.*

Dear Mr. _____:

Thank you for your letter of April 24 inquiring about a teaching position in business education at the high school level.

I regret to say that we do not now have, nor do we anticipate, any vacancy in this area for the coming year. Your letter did not indicate certification in any other field. If you are so certified, and are willing to teach in another field, please let me know. We anticipate openings in _____

I am taking the liberty of enclosing an application form and a brochure describing our district. We keep applications active for two years and we review these whenever vacancies occur. Please fill out and return to me the enclosed application form.

Thank you for your interest in our district.

Sincerely,

You may not want to include a brochure since these are fairly expensive and, at best, you are now dealing with a prospect who could be temporarily employed only in his second best level of preparation. You may prefer to wait before sending any further materials.

Administration to Candidate:

Reply to an outstanding candidate for whom you have no position.

Occasionally an outstanding application crosses your desk. The candidate towers above the rest. You may actually regret that you have no appropriate opening. The applicant may stand out because he has an unusually fine education and/or good experience. He may stand out because his is a field of short supply. Such cases need not be cause for frustration. The mails can be employed to keep track of these desirable applicants for a year or so until a vacancy occurs.

Dear Miss _____:

I regret sending a negative reply to someone who appears to be as qualified as you but we simply do not have an appropriate vacancy. At the moment we do not anticipate any vacancies in your field for next year. But changes do occur unexpectedly from time to time. Please let me know as soon as possible if you are certified in some other area and whether or not you would consider an assignment in that area. We do anticipate vacancies in

_____.

I am sending you an application blank and some literature about our district. Please complete the application, clearly indicating your second field of certification. It will probably be possible to shift you to the field of your first choice after a year or so should you accept employment in your second certification. If your only interest is in your major field, I will keep your application in our active file and notify you immediately when an appropriate vacancy occurs.

Please keep me updated on your address so that we can keep you on our mailing list. Thank you for your inquiry.

Sincerely,

Administration to Candidate:

Reply to an applicant when an appropriate vacancy exists.

The combination of an appropriate vacancy and a good candidate poses a real test of a district's methods and approaches. This is the time when the amateur operation is clearly distinguished from the professional one. The former is characterized by the disorganization which leaves letters unanswered for an inordinate period of time. The amateur approach handles correspondence in a slipshod manner. The professional approach requires that all letters be answered promptly and that they be answered well. Two days should be the longest tolerated break between the receipt of an applicant's letter and the mailing of your reply.

When the personnel administrator is on a recruiting trip, someone else must be designated to handle his correspondence. The competent secretary can answer routine correspondence. She must know such details as interview schedules, probable dates when recommended candidates will have their names presented at a board meeting, etc. if she is to handle routine correspondence. *The schedule of events for acceptance or rejection of candidates is important enough to be charted and posted in a convenient location.* Staff needs, even in the largest districts, can be similarly posted and kept current. Such procedure assures continuity of efforts even when personnel people are out of town.

The key to swift response lies in a well organized and clearly understood personnel procedure. A supply of pattern letters which the typist can copy will speed the entire operation. In a large district, form letters can achieve this end. Many of the initial inquiries can be handled by either form or pattern letters. Not *all* inquiries should be, however. *Special cases always deserve special handling.* Among these would be the filling of high administrative positions or of teaching specialties in short supply. Personal letters should be used in these cases. The administrator should make clear to his secretary which cases are to be handled which way. If another administrator is to fill in temporarily, the personnel man should spell out the entire process in writing.

The administrator who follows the procedure outlined here can service a large number of applicant letters in a day. As he goes through the mail, he should sort it into a number of piles: Those for answering with form letters, those for specific pattern letters, those for personal responses. All but the last group can be handed to a secretary with proper instructions.

Many inquiries can be handled with a simple form letter which is accompanied with some other printed materials:

Administration to Candidate:

> *Form letter to accompany application blank when a vacancy exists.*

Dear _____:

Thank you for your letter inquiring about a position as ___ _____. We do anticipate a vacancy in your field for the coming year. Enclosed is an application blank and some printed material about our district.

We regret that we must reply by a form letter but this is the time of the year when our clerks are heavily burdened with correspondence. We assure you that we are interested in candidates as individuals.

Please complete the application as soon as you can and return it to us. It would be helpful if you would ask your placement service to forward your credentials to us. We will contact you if an interview is to be arranged. Thank you for your interest in our district.

> Sincerely,

The above letter could, of course, be typed as a pattern letter if you have enough secretarial help to do so. Naturally, if it is typed, you would omit the reference to the form letter.

REPLIES TO ADMINISTRATIVE CANDIDATES

Administration to Candidate:

Early rejection.

Individual letters should be sent to all applicants for high administrative posts and to teachers bearing scarce certificates *if this is at all possible.* Sometimes, of course, a district is deluged with applications for an administrative position. In that case the screening committee (or consultants) can weed out those who do not meet the stated requirements for the position. Form replies can be sent to these:

Dear _____:

Thank you for your inquiry about our need for a new assistant superintendent for instruction.

Your letter indicates that you do not meet the following requirement: _____. We cannot, therefore, consider your candidacy in spite of your many other qualifications. Thank you again for your interest.

Sincerely,

Administration to Candidate:

Rejection after consideration.

Letters from candidates who appear to be generally qualified can be further sorted to eliminate those which show other deficiencies which will obviously lead to a negative response from the board. These deficiencies would be of a type not specifically covered by the published requirements, i.e., graduation from a college well known for its academic weaknesses, a badly written letter of application, etc. These rejects should receive a personal letter of regret which is as kind as possible.

Dear _____:

Thank you for your inquiry about our need for an assistant superintendent for instruction. We have given your candidacy serious consideration in the light of specific needs of our district and we must reluctantly exclude you from further consideration.

We are a growing district about to enter a new building program. We also plan to move into middle school organization. We must, therefore, find an administrator who has had significant middle school experience to provide the necessary leadership for this important change. We would also like the successful candidate to have had some experience in planning buildings for new programs.

These needs force us to eliminate a number of otherwise qualified people like yourself. Again, we thank you for your interest.

Very truly yours,

Either of the two preceding letters could be used for teachers carrying scarce certificates. They would need only minor revisions. Both types of applicants, the ones obviously not up to your standards and the ones unsuited by some specific requirement of your district, will crop up in the scarce teaching specialties.

Your sorting procedures will leave you with a group of administrative applicants who do meet your general and specific standards. Each of these should get a personal letter or an individually typed pattern letter. These letters should contain some details of the position and should make an effort to accomplish a soft sell.

Administration to Candidate:

Letter to those being considered.

Dear _____:

Thank you for your letter inquiring about the position of assistant superintendent for instruction. This position will be vacant upon the retirement of Dr. _____ on June 30 of this year. We are accepting applications for the position until the end of February. We will screen these early in March and hope to complete interviews by the end of that month. The successful candidate will be appointed early in April and he will be expected to begin his duties on July 1.

Dr. _____ has agreed to serve as a consultant for ten days in July to assist his successor in making a successful transition. We think this is important because of the new curricular approaches in English and science planned for September.

Enclosed are some materials about our district and our community. Please return the completed application as soon as possible. Please ask your placement service to send your credentials to us. The enclosed job description will provide you with complete information on our view of this position.

Thank you for your interest in the position and in our district.

Sincerely,

Again, with minor revisions, the above letter can be used when dealing with teachers holding scarce certificates. The revisions would delete references to the administrative position and insert particulars about the teaching job under consideration. The remarks about working with the man who is leaving might be replaced with a sentence or two about in-service education in the district.

Sometimes a special problem arises that cannot be handled conveniently in a letter. A salary agreement, for example, might still be under negotiations quite late in the year. A district might be recruiting at a time when it, or the entire state, is under NEA sanctions.

WHAT CAN YOU SAY ABOUT AN UNCERTAIN SALARY SCHEDULE?

Attitudes sometimes harden in negotiations so much that agreement is delayed until the final moment when the state mandates a completed budget. In recent years some agreements have even been delayed past that stage. It is becoming common to have an unsettled salary schedule far into that prime hiring time when the best teaching candidates are still available.

If your district has a history of low salaries, there is not much to say in recruiting materials. If, however, your history has been one of competitive salaries, reference can be made to this important fact. Facts should be cited to support the statement. As soon as tentative offers are made by the board, they can be cited as such. It is not considered cricket to retreat from such an offer with a lower one. Say so for the benefit of the novice who may not understand the emerging ground rules of board-teacher negotiations.

The best approach to the uncertain salary problem is to send out your *current* salary schedule, noting clearly and prominently that it is the current one. An addendum can be stapled to it bringing the applicant up to date on the continuing negotiations.

Administration to Candidate:

> *Salary addendum when no*
> *progress had been made to date.*

TEACHERS' SALARIES

Teachers' salaries are now under negotiations. The attached schedule is *last year's agreement*. It is the salary scale now in use. It is enclosed solely to illustrate the nature of our professional growth program. Teachers have received a raise beyond the regular step increment every year since _____. The minimum salary has been increased in each of the last _____ years. The board realizes that we must compete with surrounding districts and intends to reflect this in the final settlement.

Administration to Candidate:

> *Salary addendum when there is*
> *reported progress.*

TEACHERS' SALARIES

(Start with all of the above. Conclude with the following:)

On _____ the board offered a raise in the basic scale of $_____. If this becomes the final settlement, the beginning salary will be $_____. The lowest possible settlement under the general rules of negotiations would be the above.

It is tempting to speculate on what the final agreement will be but this must be avoided in every case even when "inside" information is available. Nothing is really final until the contract has been signed by both parties.

Teachers who are hired during negotiations will sign contracts at the old salary level. Each of these people should get a copy of the new schedule when it is adopted along with a brief form letter stating his new salary.

Administration to Candidate:

> *Form announcement of new salary scale—*
> *for those already signed to contracts.*

Dear _____:

On _____ the School Board adopted a new salary schedule to take effect in September. A copy is enclosed.

Your salary will be the one called for in the new schedule, not the one in effect when you signed your contract. Your salary will be $_____ for the coming year.

Sincerely,

A copy of the new schedule should also go to every applicant in whom you have a serious interest. A brief note should be attached:

Administration to Candidate:

Form announcement of new salary scale—
for those not signed to contracts.

Dear _____:

On _____ the School Board adopted a new salary schedule to take effect in September. A copy of this schedule is enclosed for your information. The vertical step which a teacher is on is determined by the number of years of teaching experience A teacher who is new to the district cannot, however, be placed over step 9 regardless of experience. The horizontal placement depends on graduate credits earned as indicated at the top.

Sincerely,

STATEMENT FOR USE IF THE STATE IS UNDER NEA SANCTIONS.

Sanctions have a place in American education today. Occasionally an existing evil will not be corrected unless mass coercion is applied. However, this practice is unfair to a district which is not guilty of anything except being in the state where the evil exists. The only solution to this dilemma is to face it with candor and to state the facts as clearly as possible.

Administration to Candidate:

When sanctions do not apply.

Dear _____:

As you know our State has had NEA sanctions placed upon it for what NEA called "failure to meet minimal professional salary conditions."

Typical salaries in our State are low, averaging about $_____, according to NEA's research bureau.

However, salaries in our district are not typical of the State. Our starting salary of $_____ for a BS and our maximum of $_____ for an MS are both far beyond the State averages.

They are, in fact, highly competitive with those in our neighboring states.

A copy of our salary schedule is attached. All of our teachers are on this scale at present and all will be on it next year.

We do not believe the sanctions imposed by NEA were intended for districts like ours where salary and other benefits are far beyond those which NEA found below the acceptable standards.

Sincerely,

If, as may be the case, your district is one of those obviously intended to be included in the sanctions, then your only recourse is to admit your faults and state honestly the manner in which you intend to correct them.

Administration to Candidate:

When sanctions do apply.

Dear _____ :

As you know, our State has had NEA sanctions placed upon it for what NEA called "failure to meet minimal professional salary conditions."

Typical salaries in our State are low, averaging about $_____, according to the NEA research bureau. The scale in our district, while somewhat better than the State average, has been low with a starting BS salary of $_____ and a maximum at the MS level of $_____.

Our School Board recognizes the inadequacy of this schedual. We have petitioned the Legislature and the Governor to raise State reimbursement in order to increase salaries. More important, our School Board has announced its intent to increase our salary by at least $500 at every step on the scale. The Board has indicated that this increase will be greater than $500 if increased State funds are made available for salary purposes.

We believe that this action on our part represents a responsible approach to the sanctions imposed.

Sincerely,

WHEN THE COMPLETED APPLICATION IS RECEIVED BY YOU

The purpose of all that has gone before in this chapter is to get information about the district and application forms into the hands of prospective teachers or administrators. The hope, of course, is that all those qualified will fill in the applications and mail them back to you You have some responsibility when this happens.

There are a number of things that must be done when you receive a completed application. Each requires a communication of some kind. You must: (1) let the applicant know his application has arrived in your office, (2) be certain that the applicant's placement service will forward his credentials if they have not already done so, (3) ask any specific questions not covered on the application form but now required for some reason or other, and (4) get answers to any questions the applicant may have omitted in his application.

A form letter is usually appropriate for any of these purposes and a postcard is eminently suited to achieve the first two.

Administration to Candidate:

> **Postcard to note that his**
> **application has been received**
> **in your office.**

Dear _____:

Your completed application has been received in this office. If you have not already done so, please ask your placement service to forward your credentials to us.

We shall contact you if an interview is to be arranged.

Thank you for returning the application.

Sincerely,

In the case of numbers (3) and (4) above, a separate printed form is required. Number (3) may require a special letter but it will be an unusual event so that the writing will probably not be onerous.

Never send the completed application back to the applicant *even if it is an absolute mess.* If information has been omitted, ask the applicant to furnish that information and enter it on the application yourself. If the application contains errors obviously traceable to the typing, ignore them. If errors in spelling and grammar are so bad that they reflect on the candidate's educational background, brush him off with your most polite form letter, circle the errors in bold strokes and file the application with a note to treat it with great caution.

Applications done so badly that they seem almost a mockery are becoming more common each year. The authors have seen a badly typed application returned by a candidate for a typing position. They have also read letters from would-be English teachers who have neglected to insert verbs in their sentences or who have a number of "run on" sentences in a single letter. Such an approach represents a degree of casualness that should not be encouraged by those doing the hiring.

The best approach is to ignore minor errors and treat major ones as warning signals. Omitted information on the application form may be an oversight, a simple mistake, or a deliberate thing. The only safe thing to do is to write and ask for the answers to the questions which are left unanswered.

A form letter does this best.

Administration to Candidate:

*Printed form requesting additional
information from an applicant.*

Dear _____:

Your completed application form omitted one or more of the items listed below. Would you, please, furnish the information checked below in the space provided here or, if necessary, on the reverse of this form. We will transfer it to your application form.

We lack only the item or items checked below:
Social Security number _____
Teacher Retirement number _____
Present address _____
Present phone number _____
Permanent address _____
Phone at permanent address _____
Marital status _____
Number of dependents _____
Military status _____
Graduate work _____
_____
_____

References: (1) _____
            (2) _____
            (3) _____

Other (specified) _____
_____
_____

Thank you for your cooperation in this matter.

Sincerely,

The third point listed originally, the need for some additional, and possibly unusual information, will occur rarely. When this does happen, send an individual letter as soon as possible.

Administration to Candidate:

*Asking some additional
information not usually requested.*

Dear _____:

We find that we will need a replacement for our track coach. Usually this replacement would come from our secondary school faculty but we do not seem to have anyone on our staff both qualified and interested in the position.

Though you are an applicant for an elementary school position you would not be ruled out as a possible track coach. Your application indicates that you did run on your high school and college relay teams.

Please let me know if you are interested in helping to coach the track team. Such duties would not interfere with your teaching schedule in elementary school and they would be compensated on our extra duty pay schedule.

Sincerely,

WHEN AN INTERVIEW IS DESIRED BY YOU

The best procedure in recruiting at the colleges is to send an interviewer to the scene and give him the authority to hire teachers subject to Board approval. This is important early in the season when the prime prospects are available and are being wooed like wealthy maidens. It is practical in those colleges which you normally find to be a fruitful source of candidates. For high administrative positions or for scarce teaching specialities it may be worthwhile to send your interviewer a great distance to visit one or two candidates. However, the batting average for this procedure must be good if the expenditure is to be justified.

Your recruiter, though armed with the power to issue contracts subject to Board approval, should encourage applicants to visit your area for a second interview and a personal observation of the district. This depends somewhat upon the distance involved, the importance of the position, and the training and experience of the first contact recruiter. If possible, though, the personal visit should be encouraged and the contract should not be issued until after that visit.

Some districts send out teams of teachers to recruit. This is fine for the image but teachers often lack experience in evaluation of candidates. This can create problems. Teams which include parents or students are more susceptible to the problems raised by inexperienced evaluators. Candidates discovered by such teams should be expected to visit the district before contract commitments are made. More experienced personnel can interview them then.

The visit to your home grounds can benefit the teacher who is being recruited. This, in turn, may benefit you. The teacher should see the district first hand before he signs. The authors live and work in Bucks County, Pennsylvania, the land of legend where the Broadway and writing crowd have their farms. The only problem is that we live in Lower Bucks County, a heavily urbanized bedroom for Philadelphia and New York, a place with lots of traffic and homes and no farms. A teacher who signed with us expecting the land of literary legend would be disappointed since we are located about 25 miles from the part of Bucks County he had always heard of. Far better for him to visit first, then sign—after he has seen the traffic and the urbanized area.

Interviews, then, should be arranged on your home ground if possible. The telephone is useful for arranging these, but candidates may not always be available when you can call. Letters may be required.

Administration to Candidate:
    Asking him to come for an interview.
    (1) If the applicant was interviewed away from your district.

Dear _____:

      Our recruiting team was quite impressed with your background and preparation when they visited with you on campus.

The team came home convinced that you are the sort of teacher we should seek out.

We are inviting a number of highly qualified people like yourself to visit with us for final interviews. This also will give you a chance to evaluate us.

There is a definite vacancy in _____ and we will not fill this until after the final interviews are complete. We expect to do this final interviewing during the week of _____. We could see you anytime during that week or on the Saturday before or after the close of the school week if you prefer. We suggest, however, that a visit while school is in session is best from your viewpoint.

Please fill out the enclosed stamped addressed postcard and return it to us. Select the day and time convenient to you.

We do hope you will visit us.

Sincerely,

Enclosed with this should be the postcard mentioned previously. It should be addressed to the proper person in your district and should have the proper postage on it. The name of the applicant and his field of interest should be typed in before it is sent to him.

Administration to Candidate:

Return postcard indicating interview day.

Applicant's name _____
Applicant's field _____

(circle) *Day of visit*	*Date of visit*	*Time*
Saturday	fill in	9 A.M.
Monday	"	10 A. M.
Tuesday	"	11 A.M.
Wednesday	"	noon
Thursday	"	1 P.M.
Friday	"	2 P.M.
Saturday	"	3 P.M.

Check here (   ) if no longer interested or available.

Not all applicants have been seen on college campuses or in their present teaching assignments. Some are teachers from whom you have received queries. Some of these will, sooner or later, be asked to come for an interview.

Administration to Candidate:

Asking him to come for an interview.
(2) If the applicant has not
been interviewed elsewhere.

Dear _____:

   We would like to interview you for the position of _____
_____. There is a definite vacancy for which you are quali-
fied in our _____.

   We will conduct interviews in our administration building
located at _____. A map is enclosed to help you find
it easily.

   We are conducting interviews during the week of _____
_____,including the Saturday at the close of the week. We would
like you to select a day and time convenient for you and indicate
this on the enclosed stamped addressed postcard. We suggest
that a visit while school is in session is most beneficial from the
applicant's viewpoint. This does not rule out a Saturday visit if
that is more convenient to you.

   We are looking forward to meeting you.

                                              Sincerely,

   The return postcard previously mentioned should be included
with this letter. It should contain all of the information indicated in
the previous section.

   Upon receipt of the postcard bearing the date and time of the
visit, the personnel officer should notify all administrators and
teachers who will do the interviewing. This should include the building principal if possible.

Administration to Interviewing Team:

Form used to indicate the date and time
of a scheduled interview.

Dear _____:

Miss
Mrs.
Mr.
Dr. _____, an applicant for a position in _____
_____, will arrive here at _____ A.M. on _____ for an inter-
                                     P.M.

view. You are scheduled to be on this interviewing team. Other members are: _____.
_____.

Please notify me immediately if you are unable to see the applicant at the time and date indicated. The place will be in my office.

Sincerely,

When all this has been done there remains yet one more postcard that must be sent to the applicant. He must be informed that you have received his last card and that you are expecting him for the interview.

Administration to Candidate:

*Postcard verifying appointment
for candidate's interview.*

Dear _____:

Your interview has been scheduled for ____ A.M. P.M. on
_____ as indicated by you. The interview will be held in my office in the administration building.

Please write or phone me if anything comes up to prevent your keeping this appointment.

Sincerely,

AFTER THE INTERVIEW

Too often the applicant goes home after the interview and waits and waits and waits while the School District maintains a silence glacial in the extreme. All applicants get restless under these circumstances and good ones take jobs elsewhere. The administrator should plan to alleviate this condition.

A few days after the interview a postcard should be sent to the applicant.

Administration to Candidate:

Post-interview postcard.

Dear _____:

Thank you for visiting our district last Saturday. We are now completing all interviews for the position for which you

applied and we expect to make a decision by _____.
You will be notified of our decision at that time.

Again, thank you for visiting with us.

Sincerely,

The administrator should be able to fill in the blank with a date by which he will make a decision. You should state this on the postcard as a few days after the actual decision in order to get mailed notices out to all applicants before they begin to barrage the office with phone calls.

Sometimes applicants are asked during the interview to provide some additional information. Physical education applicants, for example, might be asked for a copy of their Red Cross Life Saving Certificate. In these cases a notice should be sent to the applicant a week or so after the interview reminding him of the request. This, too, can be done on a postcard. It should be prepared individually.

Administration to Candidate:

Post-interview request (reminder)
for additional information.

Dear _____:

Just a reminder that we will need for our records a copy of your Red Cross Life Saving Certificate. We are keeping our decision open on the position awaiting receipt of this information. We will thermofax the certificate and return the original to you.

Please send it, or have it sent, as soon as possible. Thank you.

Sincerely,

WHEN YOU MUST SAY "NO"

"No" is a bad word—depressing, final, offering no hope of redemption. Repeated often enough it can crush even an ebullient person. Even said once it has an effect on morale. The administrator who must say "no" to an applicant should bear this in mind and should soften the blow as much as possible.

The *form letter* is an obvious device when saying "no" but it seems almost to compound the problem and the hurt. This is a clear case where a *pattern letter* is better since it is typed individually and is signed. Such individuality does soften the blow, especially if the writer can insert a personal touch. Naturally such personal attention is not always possible, but it is desirable if feasible.

Administration to Candidate:

The usual "no."

Dear _____:

The Personnel Committee has met and considered carefully all the applicants for the _____ position for which you applied.

Mr. _____ was selected for this position. The Committee was impressed with your background and abilities but the feeling was that Mr. _____'s greater variety of experience would best fit our needs at this time.

I am sorry that you were unsuccessful in your application. With your permission, I will keep your application on file for the next year in order to have it available if another _____ vacancy should develop.

Thank you for your interest in our district.

Sincerely,

Occasionally an outstanding candidate appears and beats out an otherwise perfectly acceptable person for the single vacancy in a particular certification field. In such cases, the administrator may want to let the unsuccessful applicant know that not only is he to be remembered but that he will be offered something soon. Such cases call for individual letters at the time plus some periodic follow-up correspondence.

Administration to Candidate:

The reluctant "no."

Dear _____:

The Personnel Committee met to consider all of the applicants for the position of _____.

Frankly, the Committee had a difficult time making a decision. Your own outstanding qualifications are one of the reasons the Committee had so much trouble.

The decision was to hire Mr. _____ who has extensive experience specifically geared to working with disadvantaged children. As you know from your interview this is a prime need with us at this time. We felt that we just had to opt for Mr. _____'s experience with disadvantaged children rather than for your strong academic work.

I would like to keep your application in our active file until an expansion occurs. May I do so? Please write and let me know. Also let me know where I can reach you in the period of the next six months or so.

Thanks for your interest in us. It was a pleasure to meet you. I hope we can get together soon.

Sincerely,

This letter lets the applicant know that he was considered something special when he finished his interview. It shows the district's reluctance to lose him and it offers a firm promise of follow up. If the follow up is done, there is a good chance that the district will get a good man for its next position and get him with relative ease.

Follow ups on prime candidates can be done easily. Their names should be added to your mailing list so that they receive copies of all of your publications as soon as these come out. They should each receive a personal note when there is some hard news to report.

Administration to Candidate:

The hard news note to prime applicants.

Dear _____:

The superintendent will propose at the next Board meeting that our _____ department be expanded. He will recommend that we add three people to the department in order to furnish additional services to our students.

One of the three new people will be specifically charged to work with underachieving students in a new program we will begin. As I recall, you did such work while on your master's program.

Would you be interested in this position if the Board approves the expansion?

Please let me know.

Sincerely,

SAYING "YES" IS A PLEASURE

Most people like to say "yes." It makes everyone feel good, especially the applicant who has been told that he is to be hired. But there are some things that should be said and some things that ought to be left out.

Among things to be said definitely are the date by which the signed contract must be returned, the teacher's assignment, if known definitely, salary, and the date on which the teacher is to report for duty. It is best to omit mention of specific building assignments unless these are absolutely certain and not subject to change.

Administration to Candidate:

Saying "yes" to the successful applicant.

Dear _____:

Congratulations.

Our Personnel Committee has selected you as the successful applicant for our _____ position. A contract, calling for a $_____ salary for ten months, will be mailed to you within a few days. Please sign both copies and return them to me before the end of this month. They will be presented to the School Board at its meeting next month (the third Thursday) and your copy will be returned to you when the Board President signs it.

Teachers new to our district are expected to report on _____ to begin a week long orientation and in-service period. As explained in your interview, you will be paid for this week. Attendance is required.

I cannot say at this time what your building assignment will be.

All of us who interviewed you were impressed with your ability and your sincere desire to work with children. We are looking forward to having you with us. Please call on me if I can be of any help to you.

Again, congratulations.

Sincerely,

A stamped, addressed postcard should be sent to the successful applicants in late May. This card should contain the applicant's name and present address and a space in which he can indicate any summer changes. Another card can be sent in early August requesting the approximate date of arrival in your area plus whatever temporary address the person will use when he first arrives. This serves to remind the teacher of his pre-service obligation. It also gives you a record of that initial local address which might prove vital in the early weeks of the school year.

USING THE DISTRICT'S NAME IN LETTERS

All of the correspondence printed in this chapter has used the words "the district," "our district," and similar terms. This may seem too impersonal for you. Maybe you prefer to use the name of your district to achieve personal identification. This is fine if the name is short and if it is one with which people identify. But if your name is "Unified District No. 37" or "The Blue Hills-West River-Urbana Joint School District," the idea loses something and the use of phrases like "the district" seems superior.

USING THE AVAILABLE PLACEMENT AGENCIES

Placement agencies come in all sizes and shapes. They do the job in every imaginable way from mediocre to excellent. They share a common trait though: They can serve your interests best when they know your needs as detailed by you. They may send applicants to you even if you send them no news but, if they do, this is a hit or miss proposition with far too high a percentage of misses.

You can avoid this scatter-gun approach with a few simple steps:

- Decide which colleges normally furnish the bulk of young teachers hired by your district and cultivate these placement officers with personal visits and personal contacts.
- Decide which colleges, now furnishing few young teachers to you, should be cultivated in an attempt to attract more of their graduates. Make personal visits here, too.
- Decide which colleges are within your recruiting sphere and get

them on your permanent mailing list. Naturally, this varies depending on the size, location and fame of your school district, but *every school district has a basic recruiting sphere,* an area where it can compete for teachers with a good chance of success. These placement directors should get your brochures, posters, news releases, and personal letters from you regarding vacancies.

- You should repeat all of these steps to determine which colleges send you the bulk of your experienced teacher candidates, which should be cultivated in an attempt to attract more, which are within your recruiting sphere.

Commercial Placement Agencies should not be overlooked. True they do charge their registrants a placement fee, but that is a matter between the registrant and the agency. It need not concern you. Good people do register with these agencies and do get placed through them. You will miss these people completely if you refuse to deal with commercial agencies as have some administrators known to the authors. Those agencies which prove unsatisfactory from your viewpoint, be they college or commercial, can be eliminated from your efforts or contacted only tangentially.

NOTIFYING THE AGENCIES

The Personal Touch

Often, as noted above, you will concentrate efforts on a few agencies that consistently send you a good number of qualified applicants. You will have established a personal relationship with the directors of these agencies. It is usually worthwhile to pen personal letters to these people. These need not be long. They need not even contain any personal references although this is not out of order if the personal reference has an appropriate tie in to your topic.

Administration to Placement Officer:

Dear _____:

Here we go again.

Our initial surveys of the faculty indicate that we will have our usual turnover in teachers for the next school year and for the same old reasons (moving from the area, promotion to administration here or somewhere else, marriage, pregnancy, etc.).

As always we would like to get to the hiring early when the best candidates are out shopping. Our salary this year is in the top 5% in the state, as you know, and our fringe benefits are the best. Negotiations are still going on but our Board has said flatly that we will not go backward in our comparative standing. That should help us.

I am sending you one of our recruiting posters under separate cover. We would be happy to have it posted on your bulletin board if there is a spot for it. The usual flood of recruiting brochures and fact sheets about the district have already been shipped to you and should arrive in a day or so.

We expect to expand our team teaching in the elementary schools next year and we will certainly give preference to teachers with training or experience in this area.

The Board has not yet approved our requests to expand the secondary school staff, but if they do, we will want to find two or three additional experienced teachers in each of the academic subjects. My personal opinion is that the growth positions will be approved.

I expect to come to the University for the State High School track championships in late April since we have a sizeable squad entered. I'd be happy to stay on for an extra day and speak to that seminar of yours again this year. I'd also be happy to speak with any interested applicants of yours at that time.

Sincerely,

The Impersonal Touch

The personal touch is not always desired or appropriate. It should be used with care. More commonly you should use the businesslike, impersonal approach. A form letter is appropriate but it is a form letter. Far better are individually typed pattern letters that state the case succinctly. These should be accompanied by copies of your brochures and fact sheet.

Dear Dr. _____:

The _____ School District anticipates the normal teacher turnover next year. As a result, we will be looking for at least fifteen elementary teachers about evenly divided between primary and intermediate. We will also need about a dozen secondary teachers in the various subjects.

Our present salary schedule begins at $_____ for the BS and goes to $_____ for the MS with _____ years experience.

We will give full credit on our salary scale for all successful teaching experience.

The enclosed brochures state our salary and fringe benefits and give detailed information about our District. Please make these available to your registrants.

Interested applicants should write directly to:
(*fill in name and address*)

Sincerely,

The Scarce Certification

The need for a teacher certified in a field that always seems in short supply (girls' physical education seems to be this way) should result in separate letters sent specifically to colleges known for their work in the required field. These letters should be brief and specific. If there are special requirements aside from the scarce certification, say so.

Dear Miss _____:

Our District needs a girls' physical education teacher for the high school. The woman who fills this position must be able to coach girls' hockey, for which she will be paid an additional sum under our extra duty pay program.

We will accept either a recent graduate or an experienced teacher. Our present salary scale runs from $_____ for the BS beginner to $_____ for the person with an MS and _____ years experience. There is an additional $_____ compensation for coaching the hockey team. The person hired for this job will be offered the opportunity to work in our summer program but will not be required to do so. This, of course, is paid additionally.

Please ask applicants to write to: (*Fill in*)

Sincerely,

In summary we can only restate our opening position. People make good schools. The central concern of all administrators should be to seek out the best possible people to teach our children and to teach our teachers. Nothing can be of greater importance to any school district. Good correspondence techniques play a positive part in getting those good people you need.

———◆———

THREE

Prevent or Solve Personnel Problems with Effective Letters

Social scientists speak about interpersonal relations; management men speak about morale; the French call it élan. Almost everyone has a name for it but the point is this: All people want to feel important, all people want to be treated as though they and their bosses are colleagues, all people care first about themselves and their own feelings, all people have sensitivities that they would like to have observed.

Whatever it may be called, it is important that the administrator attend to this human desire. Behave as though the people you deal with are wearing signs that say "I want to feel wanted." Treat them that way—with dignity, courtesy, kindness, and with firmness when needed—and they will respond in kind. Treating people like people is no more than observing the Golden Rule. Like that Biblical bread cast on the waters, it will return multifold.

Several years ago the principal of a large suburban high school started sending birthday cards to all employees in his school. The initial search for appropriate dates and addresses took time, as did the constant updating required by normal turnover in staff and changes of address. Cards were signed and addressed during the summer vacation with assistance from the principal's family. A personal touch was provided by using a wide variety of cards and by the personal signature on each one. Identical cards with printed signatures would have spoiled the effect.

The cards were signed and placed in addressed envelopes which were then stamped and sealed. All of the cards were kept in a manila folder in the principal's study at home. Appropriate reminders were placed in the desk calendar the administrator kept in his home. The man involved was in the habit of checking this calendar each morning after breakfast. Hence the reminders would send him to the manila folder to pick out the card that had to be mailed that morning in order to arrive at the staff member's home on the appropriate day.

It is impossible to assess accurately the overall results of this practice. Some people never made reference to it. Others sent notes of appreciation. Many began sending cards to the principal on *his* birthday. One brief letter of acknowledgment, however, almost justified the entire business by itself. It contained only two sentences.

> "Thanks so much for the birthday card. It was the only one I received."

Most people respond to genuine thoughtfulness. Motivational studies over the years have shown again and again that people in every level of employment work better when they feel that management really cares about them as individuals. This is becoming increasingly evident in education.

One of the major causes of current militancy is the past failures of school boards and administrators to treat teachers as human beings of consequence. Today teachers *insist* on being treated as *important* human beings; they insist that concrete evidence of such treatment must include better salaries and better working conditions as well as a voice in policy formulation and curriculum development. The administrator's responsibility must go even beyond these matters.

An effective administrator knows how to distribute praise and reprimand with justice and understanding. He takes time to learn as much as he can about each individual under his supervision. If his district is large he must turn to records for his information.

A spoken word of praise for a job well done is good. A letter is better. (Providing that it is not strong praise for weak accomplishment.) Taking time to write these in longhand lends emphasis to your thoughtfulness—unless your handwriting is illegible. Photocopies of letters of praise should always be inserted in the appropriate personnel folders.

Conversely, a reprimand should be recorded officially *only* if it follows a significant blunder or a pattern of failures which may have to lead to dismissal. These *must* be recorded accurately. Whatever its effect on the erring employee, a letter of reprimand establishes two things for the administrator: The file copy proves that the employee was fairly warned, and it remains as a potential item of evidence in case of necessary action later.

SIGNIFICANT PERSONAL EVENTS

Weddings, major anniversaries, births, and other important occasions in the lives of your school staff ought, at least, to be acknowledged by appropriate cards. There are not that many such events, even on a large staff, to excuse failure to expend the time, effort, and money for this minimal effort. In general, handwritten letters are best. They prove that you did take time to think about someone. Photocopies are easy to make if needed.

A death in the family of a friend deserves more than mere written communications. In addition to correct participation in the attendant ceremonies, a personal, handwritten letter is very appropriate. Personal references to the departed in the form of recollections of incidents may or may not be right. Some consider this poor taste. Some cherish such remembrances. If you are uncertain, omit them. The following example represents a minimal personal touch.

Administrator to Teacher:

Sympathy letter.

Dear _____:

I know that I cannot fully share the enormous loss that has come to you, but please remember that I am your friend and that all your friends are at your service in the difficult days ahead.

Would you like to have one or all of your children stay with us for a few days? If you do, please let me know.

Very sincerely,

CONTENT ANALYSIS

1. *The word* sympathy *is not used.*
2. *A specific offer of assistance is made. This means much more than "Let me know if there is anything I can do."*
3. *There is a strong statement that the mourner is not alone.*

Deaths in the family are the most obvious occasions for personal nature should get a personal note from the administrator. Such events include a serious illness suffered by the spouse of a staff member, an accident to a member of the family, natural occurences like flooding and fire. The elements of such letters should follow the suggestions offered for sympathy in time of mourning.

Administrator to Teacher:

Support for friend in time of stress.

Dear _____:

We were all extremely sorry to hear of _____'s hospitalization, but we are pleased that the problem is a relatively simple one like appendicitis. Simple or not, hospital stays are never much fun.

You must be having problems with two small children at home while mother is in the hospital. We would be happy to have you drop the children at our home on your way to work each day. They could stay with our pre-schoolers until you are ready to pick them up in the afternoon. The presence of other small children might take their minds off mother's absence.

Please let me know if you would like to do this.

With best wishes,

LETTERS OF PRAISE

A *major* assigned task, carried to completion with zeal and distinction, deserves a letter of appreciation. Professional achievements of some distinction always deserve official acknowledgment. Again, if possible, send a handwritten letter; it is more meaningful. A photocopy should be filed in the teacher's permanent folder.

CONTENT ANALYSIS

1. *There must be a clear statement of the nature and of the extent of the accomplishment.*
2. *There must be sufficient data detailed in your letter for it to become a useful part of the person's personnel folder.*
3. *You must make specific citations of fact to support judgment statements.*
4. *When appropriate, encourage further activities of the same type.*

Administrator to Teacher:

Congratulations on completed graduate work.

Dear _____:

Congratulations on being granted the M.Ed. degree in guidance by _____ University.

I know well how much effort and persistence was involved in accomplishing this on a part-time basis. I also know the financial sacrifice you made in fulfilling the one semester, full-time internship.

Your thesis, I have been told, explored some new approaches to guidance at the elementary level. I would like to read it.

You will, of course, be placed on the master's salary schedule as soon as you present the required verifications on your *Salary Adjustment Form.* My secretary will send you the forms.

Sincerely,

Administrator to Teacher:

Congratulations on publication.

Dear _____:

I was interested in your article entitled "A Flexible Approach to Cafeteria Scheduling in a Large High School" in the _____ issue of the _____.

Do you think we could try your "free flow" plan at _____ High next year? Why don't you talk it over with Mr. _____, the Cafeteria Manager, to get his angles on it?

Publication in a national professional journal reflects credit to our District as well as to you, the author.

Congratulations.

Sincerely,

Administrator to Teacher:

Praise for completion of a major committee assignment.

Dear _____:

I would like to thank you for your outstanding service this year as chairman of the social studies committee. I have read the excellent report and I congratulate you and the committee for the significant recommendations and the thorough research which provided the supportive evidence.

I know how many hours of hard work are represented by this document and I assure you that each recommendation will be carefully considered by the administration and by the Board of Education.

Thanks, again, for a job well done.

Sincerely,

We assume, of course, that the statements in the letter are *true*. We also assume that appropriate individual acknowledgments should go to the committee members. It follows, of course, that the above letter will become a farce if the report is filed and forgotten. All educators are understandably sensitive to "file and forget" practices. Had the report deserved such a fate, the letter should never have been written. If segments of the recommendations cannot be implemented for reasons beyond administrative control, another letter should be written.

Administrator to Teacher:

*Explanation for failure to follow through
on committee recommendations.*

If the committee recommendations are not sound, say so, substantiate your statements, but try to salvage something to avoid a complete loss of face for the committee. If outside factors hold up implementation, say so with a brief explanation.

Dear _____:

As I promised in my letter following the presentation of the excellent recommendations of your committee, I have made every effort to follow through on implementation.

The administrative staff supported my recommendations to the School Board for additional funds for the necessary books and materials. A recent cut in state support, however, restricts the actions of the Board at this time. I am certain that you understand the priority of salary increases for next year.

There never seems to be enough money to do the things we want to do in our schools when we want to do them.

Please assure your committee that all of its recommendations will remain in my active file.

Sincerely,

Sometimes less overwhelming achievements deserve letters of praise. An unusual extracurricular program might rate such a letter as, for example, the teacher who undertakes to direct a serious Broadway play instead of the usual high school trivia. He would certainly deserve praise if he carries it off successfully. There are times, such as the foregoing, when failure might rate hurrahs for effort alone. A particular unusual and worthwhile teaching unit (or individual lesson) also deserves a personal note.

Administrator to Teacher:

Praising a good teaching unit.

Dear _____:

Your recently completed unit on local government deserves praise, particularly for its wise use of consultants and for its well planned and appropriate field trips.

Having the heads of major departments of the city government visit your class as resource persons and following each of these appearances with class visits to the departments involved represents a fine combination of practice and theory.

There is probably a potential article for a professional magazine in the approach you used.

Again, congratulations.

Sincerely,

Administrator to Teacher:

Praising an outstanding student performance.

Dear _____:

Saturday's performance of _____ was one of the finest high school productions I have seen. Your courage in undertaking a serious and signfcant play with adolescent talent must be admired. I agree with your obvious feelings that too much trivia is presented by high school groups.

The evidence of your fine direction was obvious throughout

the performance. The young people on and off stage were a credit to their director.

Thank you for a fine evening of *good* theatre.

Sincerely,

Administrator to Teacher:

Thanking him for a public relations contribution.

When a staff member reflects credit to the District in some type of public appearance or presentation, he deserves a letter of thanks that will encourage more of the same.

Dear _____:

I was pleased to hear that you made a fine presentation to the _____ PTA on our new remedial reading program in the secondary schools. My informant tells me that your tape recording of the "before and after" skill demonstrations was especially effective.

The community understanding resulting from your speech should help us greatly when we expand the reading program next year.

Would you care to speak to other groups on the same topic later in the year?

Sincerely,

Earlier we warned of hasty and excessive written praise for weak accomplishments. Without retracting that advice, we want to point out that a weak teacher can often be improved by judicious praise offered in a positive manner. Find something which he does well, praise it honestly, and offer a suggestion by which he can use this as a springboard to further success.

Administrator to a Weak Teacher:

Praising an accomplishment.

Dear _____:

The afternoon session you conducted for three students who asked for help with the binomial theorem was as impressive as it was helpful to the students.

I liked what I saw when I dropped in on the session. The students apparently profited from the time you gave them and went home with a sound mastery of an important mathematical concept. This was a good piece of work.

I would like to suggest something which may help transfer this skill to a larger group.

When you teach your sixth period Basic Math course, why not select four or five of your poorest students and pretend you are teaching only to them, one at a time. Shift to each one in turn, using the same questioning techniques you used with the smaller group. It may not work immediately, but why not give it a chance —at least for one full period?

Again, I think the afternoon session was an indication of what you really can do.

Sincerely,

EXPRESSIONS OF GRATITUDE
TO RETIRING TEACHERS

When one honors a retiring teacher, one honors the profession. Appropriate ceremonies are the responsibility of the retiree's colleagues and of the administrators who have worked with him. At a minimum, a retiree should receive, in addition to whatever gifts and honors are considered appropriate and customary in the area, letters from the following school people:

1. All close friends;
2. A representative teacher speaking for the staff of the school in which the teacher works;
3. The principal of every school in the district in which the teacher has worked;
4. The President and Executive Committee of the Teachers' Association;
5. The School Board;
6. The Chief Administrator of the district.

CONTENT ANALYSIS

All of these letters should differ, of course, but each should contain, in its own way, four elements:
1. Congratulations in a cheerful, positive manner;
2. Reference to the number of years of service in the school or in the district;

3. *Reference to particularly significant achievements; each such reference should be appropriate to the group represented by the writer;*
4. *Reference to the activity plans of the teacher in retirement.*

May we add that in most cases a traveling bag is a more appropriate gift than an easy chair.

Teachers' Group to Retiring Colleague:

Dear _____:

All of the teachers in the _____ School District extend to you our congratulations and our gratitude for your thirty-five years of service to the children, to the district, and to our profession.

Your contributions for seven years to the _____ Education Association as chairman of the membership committee will be long remembered. Your presidency of the Association for two years during a particularly crucial period was instrumental in shaping our present negotiations procedures.

We hope that you will maintain regular contact with our organization and that you will find great satisfaction in the travel experiences you are planning. We would enjoy your sharing these with us when you return. Bon Voyage!

Gratefully,

Administrator to a Teacher:

Leaving the district after long service.

Dear _____:

Congratulations on your appointment to an assistant professorship at _____ Community College. I wish we could have retained you at _____ High School, but I know that you deserve broader academic challenges at a higher level.

Thank you sincerely for twelve years of outstanding service to the youth of _____. I thoroughly enjoyed the yearbooks produced under your guidance. Perhaps, if your duties permit, we can ask you to return from time to time as a consultant and lecturer in our humanities course. I understand that this will be your specialty at _____.

Good luck.

Sincerely,

RETIRING BOARD MEMBERS

School board membership is one of the most demanding and thankless chores assumed by volunteers in our nation. Board members are subject to criticism and often abuse from all sides, particularly when they display principles and courage. Is it too much to expect that letters of thanks for voluntary service be sent to them when they complete their services? Is it appropriate to ignore them simply because we may have disagreed with some of their positions? We think not. In this case, the letter of appreciation can contain the same elements illustrated above.

Administrator to a Retiring Board Member:

Dear _____:

Let me extend my personal and sincere thanks for your eight years of service to the children of _____ by membership on our School Board.

I am particularly grateful for your support and for your contributions of sound ideas in our recent building program. Whenever you pass _____ High School you can take pride in your significant part in making this particular dream a reality.

I know you will enjoy spending more time with Alice and the boys free of constant telephone calls, pressures exerted by various individuals and groups, and lengthy evening meetings.

Cordially,

LETTERS OF REPRIMAND

CONTENT ANALYSIS

All letters of reprimand should contain the following elements:
1. *A specific charge or charges including time, date and location;*
2. *A clear statement of the evidence supporting the charges;*
3. *A clear statement of what is expected by way of improvement;*
4. *An indication of any time limitations involved;*
5. *A reference of action may be necessary if improvement is not evidenced within the stated time limit which is needed for serious cases or for repeated minor offenses.*

Administrator to Non-Professional Employee:

Reprimand for unsatisfactory performance.

Dear _____ :

In the past three weeks I have received reports from Mr. _____, our Maintenance Foreman, stating that your work has been completely unsatisfactory on a major project assigned to you.

You were directed to paint the bleachers at the_____ Memorial Baseball Field on Wednesday, _____. The job sheet clearly indicates that three coats were to be applied before October 15th.

As you know, the weather has been ideal for painting. I inspected the bleachers today (October 16th) and found evidence of only one coat of paint. In addition to this you had spilled a quantity of paint on the cement ramp leading to the field house.

Mr. _____ further states that this quality of workmanship has been typical of most jobs you have done since you were hired in September.

Unless you begin to show us immediately that you can do a better job of painting, you will be transfered to the Grounds Crew at a reduction in rating and salary to Laborer, Class II.

I enclose a photostatic copy of the job sheet. You are directed to complete the two additional coats on the bleachers in a good, workmanlike manner before October 31st, weather permitting.

Very truly yours,

Reprimand to a Teacher:

For excessive absenteeism.

Dear _____ :

Our records show that you have been absent on the following 23 days since school opened in September (*list them*). All but two of the absences were on Mondays or Fridays. Your principal reports that he spoke to you on four occasions about this problem and that your responses were vague and unsatisfactory.

The number and the pattern of these absences makes it necessary that I request a physician's verification under our policy

#4931.3. You may refer to this policy on page 603 of the District's policy book which may be obtained from your principal's secretary.

I need not remind you of the negative effect of excessive teacher absenteeism on students.

Reports indicate that your teaching performance is satisfactory. I would like to recommend you for tenure, but I cannot do this unless your attendance record improves.

Very truly yours,

DISMISSAL OF A TENURE TEACHER

Tenure laws are generally misunderstood. Although they vary from state to state, none are really intended to prevent the dismissal of an *incompetent* teacher. They provide an orderly procedure which protects the rights of an individual teacher and which requires the employer to prove his case beyond a reasonable doubt.

While it is clear that these laws, *in practice,* have the effect of protecting incompetents, especially emotionally unstable teachers, the fault is usually not with the law itself but rather with administrators and school boards. This is due to:

1. Inadequate supervision which fails to correct the faults of the teacher;
2. Inadequate records which fail to substantiate the charges or demonstrate that sufficient corrective measures were taken;
3. An unwillingness to go through the anguish, the trouble, and the expense of carrying the case through the possible stages (at least three) of appeal with all the attendant bad publicity.

The last point is not the least to be considered. Nobody praises the school board for thinking of the welfare of children when an incompetent teacher is dismissed and decides to fight the case. More often there is created an emotional atmosphere not unlike that of a landlord-tenant battle. No matter what the facts are, the underdog is always right. Few have the insight to understand that, in this case, the underdog may be the child who is being subjected to bad teaching, or even worse.

We do not feel that a pattern letter can be developed here because of the tremendous differences in each case and because of variations in the laws of the 50 states. On the other hand, we can offer guidelines and a content analysis of the letter which goes to the teacher about to be dismissed.

GUIDELINES

1. Every possible alternative must be tried before formal dismissal procedures. The chief administrator should have evidence that frequent and reasonable attempts to correct the teacher have been adequately recorded. Mixed evaluations by supervisors may not be detrimental to the case but the specific charges must stand up in court if necessary.
2. Consultation with the School Board attorney is essential before any steps are taken.
3. All the facts must be presented to the School Board. Without their backing, the case is closed. If the administration spokesman cannot convince the board, he can hardly convince a court of appeal.
4. The teacher should be offered the alternative of a quiet resignation. Ideally, only the chief administrator and the teacher would be involved. Otherwise there is no advantage to the teacher. However, if formal dismissal is given as the alternative, the administrator must be prepared to carry it out if a resignation is refused. If he fails to do so, this avenue will be closed in the future. Idle threats which are not carried out quickly become futile.

Perhaps the day will come when the teaching profession will create a "bar association" which can examine evidence in potential dismissals and hopefully help rid the profession of incompetents. Unfortunately, the official stance of teacher organizations today seems to be that no teacher is ever incompetent. The administrator cannot ethically state his side of the case to his teacher organization until formal proceedings are held. The teacher, however, can tell his side to all who listen. Propaganda from one side and silence from the other, combined with normal pro-teacher/anti-administration bias, can build great sympathy for the teacher involved. The result, often, is that the professional organization will back the teacher regardless of the degree of his incompetency unless he is convicted of a civil crime. The administrator must consider this factor.

When it is determined that the evidence is clear, when a resignation has been refused, when the board and their attorney agree to go ahead with formal dismissal, then the chief administrator must prepare a letter (to be reviewed by the attorney) which should contain the following elements:

CONTENT ANALYSIS

1. *The exact charges must be stated, using the specific terms spelled out in the state law as proper reasons for dismissal of the teacher;*
2. *The time and date of a school board hearing must be indicated;*
3. *The teacher's right, under law, to representation must be defined;*
4. *An anecdotal record must be included. This should contain a chronological outline of the evidence supporting the charges; along with this should be a record of attempts made by his supervisors to correct the teacher;*
5. *There must be referrals to specific laws, policies and regulations violated; the record must show that these were pointed out to the teacher at least once during the period in question.*

Other elements may be required by the laws of the state involved, but the above guidelines and elements are applicable anywhere since they are based on considerations of the civil rights of an American citizen. It seems clear at this point that the district which attends properly to its correspondence is the district best prepared to handle an extreme situation. As we noted earlier: "An angry letter written in haste may turn up as evidence in court or as a source document at a school board hearing. A hasty memo offering too much praise for a routine accomplishment may take on great importance. . . ."

We offer no further comment.

FOUR

———◆———

Letters Dealing with
School Business Functions

Good teachers make good schools. This cannot be repeated too often, especially when considering the necessary elements of bureaucracy that form the running gears of a school district. We are not ignoring the engine. We merely say that as an engine will not provide reliable transportation without good tires, wheels, brakes, etc., so teachers must have adequate buildings, supplies and equipment. The central teaching function must be supported by a wide variety of efficient ancillary services.

The nerve center of most of this network of services is the school district business office. In larger districts a high ranking staff administrator, with appropriate supervisory assistance, assumes the major responsibility for all these services. In smaller districts they will represent a portion of the job of the assistant superintendent or of the superintendent himself.

A great deal of paperwork and correspondence is involved in the business operation. Unfortunately, *it does not decrease in volume in proportion to the decrease in size of the district*. Thus, in the small district, it is absolutely essential to streamline the drudgery of business correspondence.

Money is the current that lights up a school district. Most business correspondence involves money in some way. That makes business correspondence extremely important to a school district. The letters you write will often quote dollar amounts or cite purchase specifications. They must contain no errors or ambiguities. Thus, they should *never be mailed until they are proofread* by the responsible administrator. Letters, as noted earlier, have a way of turning up in court.

Careful phrasing and *proofreading before* mailing cannot be overemphasized in preparing business letters. These precautions cannot be delegated down the chain of command, even in the largest district. Remember that you are dealing with an easily measured commodity—money—and you are dealing with it right out in the open where everyone can see you.

This chapter has been organized into four areas:

> *The Confirming Letter*
> *Financial Affairs*
> *Management*
> *The Spotlight Items: Food and Bus Operations*

THE CONFIRMING LETTER

Not too long ago we had an experience in which attention to our recommended rules saved embarrassment and higher costs. A teacher was contracted to teach a course pending NDEA funding. The initial contacts were made by telephone. The tentative nature of the position was stressed to the prospective teacher. It was clearly stated there would be no job unless the federal funding came through. The teacher said that he understood.

Fortunately we followed our own rules, the first of which is to send confirming letters after any oral communications that promise jobs or imply costs, contracts, or that something will be done.

Confirming letters have their own rationale. They must be concise. They must spell out the agreements reached orally. They must promise nothing directly or indirectly beyond that which was agreed to in the initial conversations. They must be mailed promptly, within a day, or at most two, of the oral arrangements. They should ask the recipient to respond in writing if your letter *does not* state the agreement exactly. This last point is essential. Specify that the recipient write to you if any corrections are needed; thus, the absence of any written answer implies that your letter is correct as written and this can be an important point as it was in the case under discussion.

Business Administrator to Teacher:

Confirming conditions of agreement to teach a special course.

Dear _____:

This letter is to confirm our telephone conversation of September 11, 19__.

The School District has *tentatively* scheduled a sixteen week institute in astronomy. If offered, the institute will begin on January 8, 19__ and run for sixteen (16) weeks, meeting once a week. Each class will meet from 4:00 to 6:00 P.M.

We have applied for NDEA funding for this project and the institute is offered subject to that funding. If we are funded, we would like you to serve as instructor with salary and expenses according to NDEA scale. We will register our students for this program on a tentative basis. We will know in early December if we are to be funded and we will then inform you definitely about your employment.

Please let me know by letter if this arrangement is satisfactory to you.

Sincerely,

CONTENT ANALYSIS

1. *There is a referral to a specific telephone conversation.*
2. *There is a specific description of the offer.*
3. *There are repeated referrals to limitations and the tentative nature of the offer.*
4. *There is a date of final decision.*
5. *There is a request for written confirmation.*

In the case described above, the funding was not realized and the teacher was so notified. We were shocked to receive from him a bill for the services he was prepared to render and a letter stating that the absence of funding did not affect his position because he was prepared to teach the course.

Without our copy of the confirming letter we would have had one of those interesting cases in which two parties relate differing recollections of a telephone conversation. In this case, however, the ending was different.

Business Administrator to Teacher:

Citing confirming letter as a basis for a void claim for pay for services not rendered.

Dear _____:

Your letter of December 5, 19__ and the attached bill came as a surprise to us. Our agreement was tentative and subject to availability of NDEA funds. This was made clear to you in a letter dated September 11, 19___. A copy is attached. You did not respond negatively.

Under these conditions we do not intend to pay your bill.

Sincerely,

We heard no more.

FINANCIAL AFFAIRS

The financial sector of the business operation includes financial planning, accounting and auditing, insurance, debt service, cost analysis and related bidding functions. These operations in some way involve all district employees at one time or another. They also involve various vendors, other governmental and public or private agencies, and the public. Thus, the people with whom you correspond will represent wide ranges of intelligence, education, and experience.

No single rule will enable you to write prose which is universally appropriate. Restating some of the advice outlined in Chapter One,

- Keep it simple and clear. Always try to use the short word if it does the job.
- Avoid technical terms and educational jargon wherever possible.
- Strive for shorter, simpler sentences.
- Try to cover each topic in as few words as possible but do not fear repetition if heavy emphasis is necessary.
- Remember that a letter covering one topic is a good letter because it can be easily filed.
- Rewrite the original letter at least once.

LETTERS TO EMPLOYEES

Supervisory letters to employees are covered in Chapter Three. Business letters to employees generally concern money. These letters or memos should be brief, clear, and accurate. Except in unusual cases, form letters should be prepared for this type of communication. The form letter should include clear statements of the following:

1. The amount of money involved.
2. The length and nature of the service to be performed.
3. Any limitations, uncertainties, or unusual contingencies involved.

4. The name and title of the person to contact if any questions arise.

5. The procedure to follow in case of administrative error.

These form letters can be personalized if desired by individually typed names and personal signatures.

Business Administrator to Teachers:

Indicating salary changes.

Dear _____:

The School Board and the Teachers' Association have agreed on a new salary schedule to become effective September 19__. A copy of this schedule is attached.

Our records indicate that you are presently on step _____ of the _____ scale. You will move in September to step _____ of the _____ scale. Your annual salary in September will be $_____. This includes only your basic teaching salary. Extra activities which receive compensation will be paid under separate contracts and will not affect your pension fund or withholding for income tax purposes. You should consider this when you plan ahead for your federal and state income tax levies. *We do not deduct from supplementary pay for income tax purposes.*

If you believe our records to be in error, please contact Mr. _____, our Personnel Director, so that the matter can be verified and corrected, if necessary. You should also notify his office by our *Graduate Credit Form* of courses you have completed recently so that our records can be updated.

Sincerely,

Business Administrator to Teacher:

Requesting information for salary purposes.

Dear _____:

Our records show that you have completed _____ credits beyond the _____ degree.

We are now in the process of updating and verifying our personnel records. Would you please fill in the attached form and return it to the business office before _____.

Thank you for your cooperation.

Sincerely,

TEACHER'S STATEMENT OF SALARY INFORMATION FORM

Name (please print) _____

School Assigned _____

Circle Highest Completed Degree
Level

    BS   MS   EdD

Do you have credits beyond the
highest completed degree? (circle)

    YES   NO

If yes, how many? _____

Years (including current one) experience in this district _____

Years experience elsewhere _____

FOR OFFICE USE ONLY

**VERIFICATION OF CREDITS
BY TRANSCRIPT ON FILE**

Name of Verifier   Date

_____

**VERIFICATION OF EXPERI-
ENCE BY LETTERS ON FILE**

Name & Title		
of Verifying	School	
Official	District	Date

Name of Person Checking Experience Verification

_____

Date of Experience Check _____

_____

Please explain extent and reasons for partial years. _____
_____
_____

Are you now taking graduate work? (circle)   YES   NO
If yes, how many hours? _____
Do you plan to take graduate work next semester or next summer? (circle)
      YES   NO
If yes, how many hours? _____

     Business Administrator to Teacher:

       Request for additional salary information.

Dear _____:

     Your recently submitted salary information form indicates
that you have completed _____ hours beyond your _____ degree. The records on file with us do not support this.

     We have transcripts from _____
_____.

These show a _____ degree plus _____ graduate hours.

Would you, please, request your university to send us transcripts for that work of which we have no record.

Thank you.

Sincerely,

Business Administrator to Teacher:

Stating conditions for a fringe benefit.

Dear _____:

By agreement, the Board of School Directors has provided all employees a life insurance policy with a face value of _____.

To be placed on the active rolls for this policy, the insurance company requires that you be in the employment of the school district for a continuous period of three (3) months. These rolls are brought up to date at the beginning of each month.

Effective _____, your name will be added to the insurance roll.

So that records are up to date, kindly complete the enclosed card [*See Figure 1*] and return it to Mr. _____'s office as soon as possible.

Sincerely,

Business Administrator to Teacher:

Stating a claim procedure for a fringe benefit.

Dear _____:

The following procedures are to be followed in the event that you become injured while working for the school district.

1. Report your injury immediately to your supervisor and to the business office.

2. Forward all bills relating to your injury *directly* to the business office. This includes all doctor, hospital, medical and prescription bills.

3. Contact Mr. _____ should any problems arise from your claim.

Sincerely,

GROUP INSURANCE ENROLLMENT AND RECORD CARD

PLEASE PRINT ALL ANSWERS

CLOCK OR CHECK NUMBER

NAME					MALE	FEMALE
	LAST NAME	FIRST NAME	MIDDLE INITIAL			

RESIDENCE				
	Street	City	State	

OCCUPATION

DEPARTMENT

DATE BORN			DATE EMPLOYED			SINGLE ☐	WIDOWED ☐
Month	Day	Year	Month	Day	Year	MARRIED ☐	DIVORCED ☐

My Beneficiary (Example: Mary A. Doe, not Mrs. John J. Doe)

INITIAL AMOUNT OF INSURANCE
According to Plan

		EMP.	DEP.*
LIFE			
ACC. DEATH & DISMEMBERMENT			
WEEKLY ACC. & SICK. BENEFIT			
LONG TERM DIS. MO. BENEFIT			
HOSPITAL, SURG. BENEFITS, ETC.			
MAJOR MEDICAL			

	RELATIONSHIP
FIRST NAME　MIDDLE INITIAL　LAST NAME	

RESIDENCE OF BENEFICIARY			
Street	City	State	

If more than one beneficiary is designated, settlement will be made in equal shares to such of the designated beneficiaries (or beneficiary) as survive the Insured, unless otherwise provided herein.

If no designated beneficiary survives the Insured, settlement will be made to the Estate of the Insured, unless otherwise provided in the Group Policy.

*LIST ALL ELIGIBLE DEPENDENTS ON REVERSE SIDE OF CARD

If contributions are required under this Plan, I authorize my employer to deduct from my earnings until further notice my contributions for insurance under a policy issued by The Prudential Insurance Company of America.

Employer...

Date..................., 19......　...　*Signature of Employee*

(Sign Full Name)

FOR EMPLOYER'S USE ONLY (Continued on back)

CERTIFICATE NO.		EFFECT. DATE OF INS.

Figure 1

Names of Eligible Dependents	Relationship	Date of Birth	Effective Date

CHANGES OF BENEFICIARY (EMPLOYER'S USE ONLY)

Date of Change	New Beneficiary Designated	Relationship

CHANGED AMOUNT OF INSURANCE

	Eff. Date	Amount	Eff. Date	Amount	Eff. Date	Amount	Eff. Date	Amount	Cert. Canc.	Cert. Reins.	Cert. Canc.
Life											
Acc. Death and Dism.											
Acc. & Sick.											
LTD											

ORD 8822 WD ED 9-67

Printed in U.S.A. by Prudential Press

Reprinted courtesy of The Prudential Insurance Company

Figure 1 (reverse)

Business Administrator to Teacher:

Stating procedure for optional payroll deduction.

Dear _____:

U.S. Savings Bonds may be purchased through payroll deductions by any employee regularly employed by the school district.

Deductions are made only in the amounts of $9.38, $18.75, and $37.50 from each payroll check except in those months where there are three pay dates. *Authorization continues from year to year unless cancelled.* Bonds are issued by the National Bank of _____.

All persons who desire this service at this time should fill in the Authorization Form below and return it to their school office on or before September 20, 19__. Bond designation cards will be sent to you to be completed.

Authorizations are opened only twice during the school year, September and March, to go into effect the following month.

Sincerely,

PAYROLL DEDUCTION
Authorization

To: School District of _____

I, the undersigned, hereby authorize you to deduct from my wages each pay the sum of $_____ (fill in the amount $9.38, $18.75, or $37.50). This will be deducted from each payroll check except in those months where there are three pay dates. Deductions will be made from only two paychecks in any month since the bank is notified on a monthly basis to purchase U.S. Savings Bonds. Deductions are to commence with the first pay of October, 19__.

I agree that this Authorization shall continue from year to year unless I notify the payroll department in writing to stop further deductions. Such notice must be at least thirty (30) days prior to the effective date of cancellation.

I further agree that all said bonds shall be issued in the name (names) and address listed on the bond designation card. Notification of change will be given, in writing, at least thirty (30) days prior to the effective date of change.

_____

PRINT or TYPE name
_____

Signature
_____

Date

Business Administrator to Teacher:

  Accompany fringe benefit claim form.

Dear _____:

Our records indicate that you attended graduate school last semester.

As you know, the District reimburses teachers to an annual limit of _____ for graduate tuition.

Attached is a copy of the reimbursement form. Please complete this and return it to Mr. _____'s office as soon as possible.

Thank you.

Sincerely yours,

APPLICATION FOR REIMBURSEMENT FOR GRADUATE STUDY
(Submit in Duplicate)

To Be Completed by Employee
Name _____ School _____ Date _____
Home
Address _____
Type of Certificate _____
Subjects Certified to Teach _____
Amount of Reimbursement Requested $_____
Attach the Following

  1. Catalogue description of   3. Transcripts
     course(s)   4. Description of your par-
  2. Evidence of Cost   ticipation and contribu-
                                     tion of the course(s)

University	Dates of Attendance	Number	Course(s) Pursued Name of Course	Credit Hours	Grade

To Be Completed by the Building Principal
Teacher's major teaching assignment _____
How does this course work contribute to the effectiveness of the
teacher in his teaching assignment? _____
_____
_____

Approved _____ Not Approved _____ Date _____
To Be Completed by the District Superintendent
Not Approved _____ Date _____
Approved _____ Amount _____ Date _____

Business Administration to Staff:

Memo or letter stating working conditions.

To: All Principals and Office Personnel
From: _____, Administrative Assistant to the
          Superintendent in Charge of Business Affairs
Date: April 8, 19__

1. Effective Monday, June 17, 19__, all school offices will be
   open between the hours of 8:00 A.M. and 4:00 P.M. Offices
   will be closed for lunch for one-half hour from 12:00 to
   12:30 P.M. Secretaries may leave the building during this
   time.

2. Effective Monday, June 17, 19__, the mail run will leave
   the Administration Building at 8:30 A.M. each day.

3. Offices may close at 3:00 P.M. on July 3, 19__, August 30,
   19__, and December 31, 19__.

4. Schedule of paid holidays for Office Personnel:
Independence Day	— July 4
Labor Day	— September 2
Thanksgiving	— November 28, 29
Christmas	— December 24, 25
New Year's Day	— January 1
Easter	— April 4, 7
Memorial Day	— May 30

5. Beginning September 3, 19__, the Administrative Offices will
   resume operating from 8:30 A.M. to 4:30 P.M.

LETTERS TO VENDORS

Correspondence with vendors, both actual and potential, involves large sums of money in the aggregate. Efficiency in this realm is

achieved by attention to detail in each instance. Carelessness in these letters can cause untold embarrassment for the school district and might result in serious financial loss. The cautions offered at the beginning of the chapter are especially applicable here.

LETTERS SOLICITING BIDS

These letters, or notices, must:
- be inclusive enough to describe the item to be bid;
- deal with related items or be confined to a single item;
- state the date by which bids must be submitted;
- state the place to which bids must be submitted;
- state any special conditions attached to the bid;
- state the time and place of opening and award;
- state the conditions under which all bids will be rejected and a re-bidding process begun.

The various states have hedged the bidding process with legal requirements, which vary from state to state. The best approach is for you to ascertain those in effect in your state. The sample bid solicitation which follows meets Pennsylvania requirements.

SCHOOL DISTRICT OF BRISTOL TOWNSHIP
800 Coates Avenue
Bristol, Pennsylvania

January 19___

The School District of Bristol Township invites bids on the Collection of Refuse according to the attached specifications.

This bid form must be submitted in a sealed envelope, marked on the outside "Bid on the Collection of Refuse," and mailed or delivered to Mrs. _____, Secretary, School District of Bristol Township, 800 Coates Avenue, Bristol, Pennsylvania 19007. All bids must be received by 4:00 P.M. Monday, January 6, 19___. Bids will be opened at 7:30 P.M. January 6, 19___ in the Harry S. Truman Administration Building, 800 Coates Avenue, Bristol, Pennsylvania.

The awarding of bids will be made at a meeting of the Board of School Directors within sixty days of the opening of bids.

The Board of School Directors reserves the right to reject any or all bids, reject or accept any individual item when more than one item is bid, and to accept an adjusted quantity at a price per unit determined by dividing the quantity provided in the request for bids into the total price as appears on the bid for the item in question.

In the event that all bids are unacceptable, the Board of School Directors will invite new bids within a period of sixty days.

BY _____

Signature of Bidder

_____

Name of Firm

_____

Address of Firm

_____

Telephone Number

SCHOOL DISTRICT OF BRISTOL TOWNSHIP

Specifications for Refuse Collection, School Year 19___–19___

1. All refuse shall be collected at all the schools listed below.
2. All refuse shall be picked up on a regular time schedule on each day school is in session.
3. Hours of collection shall be between 2:30 P.M. and 5:00 P.M.
4. The Contractor shall be solely responsible for Workmen's Compensation and Public Liability Insurance.
5. Payment shall be made monthly upon submission of a bill listing the number of pick-ups for the month.
6. Bidder must furnish the name and address of three concerns for whom he has done work in the past year.
7. Bid must be on bid form attached.

BRISTOL TOWNSHIP SECONDARY SCHOOLS:

1. Benjamin Franklin Junior High School, 6401 MillCreek Road, Levittown
2. Delhaas High School, 1200 Rogers Road, Bristol
3. Franklin Delano Roosevelt Jr. High School, 1001 Rogers Road, Bristol
4. Woodrow Wilson High School, 3001 Green Lane, Levittown

BRISTOL TOWNSHIP ELEMENTARY SCHOOLS:

1. Clara Barton School, Blue Ridge Drive & Blue Lake Road, Levittown

2. James Buchanan School, 2200 Haines Road, Levittown
3. George Clymer School, 4401 Sunset Avenue, Newportville
4. Mary W. Devine School, 1800 Keystone Avenue, Croydon
5. Mary W. Devine School Annex (St. Luke's Lutheran Church, 1305 State Road, Croydon)
6. Ralph Waldo Emerson School, 6501 MillCreek Road, Levittown
7. John Fitch School, Greenbrook Drive & Field Lane, Levittown
8. Thomas Jefferson School, Appletree Drive, Levittown
9. Lafayette School, 4201 Fayette Drive, Bristol
10. Abraham Lincoln School, 10 Plumtree Place, Levittown
11. Maple Shade School, 2335 Prospect Avenue, Croydon
12. George Washington School, 275 Crabtree Drive, Levittown.

SCHOOL DISTRICT OF BRISTOL TOWNSHIP
800 Coates Avenue
Bristol, Pennsylvania

_____
                                               Date

BID FORM—Refuse Collection
School Year, 19___–19___
    The _____ guarantees
                     Name of Firm
to collect all refuse at all the Bristol Township Schools each day
Monday through Friday when school is in session for the sum of
_____ per individual pick-up.

    TOTAL BID for estimated 182 collections _____

Listed below are the names of three firms for whom the undersigned has done work during the past year.

Name of Firm	Address	Telephone No.
Name of Firm	Address	Telephone No.
Name of Firm	Address	Telephone No.

                           BY _____
                           Signature of Bidder
                           _____
                           Name of Firm
                           _____
                           Address of Firm
                           _____
                           Telephone Number

Business Administrator to Vendor:

Announcing bid award.

Gentlemen:

At the meeting last night the _____ School Board accepted your bid of $_____ for the following item(s):

# or amt.	item	del. place	del. date

Prompt delivery to the designated place is essential. Please notify us immediately if, for any reason, you are unable to meet a delivery deadline. Bills rendered after delivery will be paid at the next School Board meeting.

Sincerely,

Business Administrator to Vendor:

Rejecting a bid.

This can and should be a form letter which goes to all unsuccessful bidders. You should include a statement of the reason for rejection or an explanation for choice of the successful bidder. A mention of inclusion on lists to be solicited for future bids is helpful.

Gentlemen:

the following reason(s): _____
_____.
_____.

The successful bidder was _____
with their bid of _____.

Your name is included in the list of those to be solicited for bids on this item in the future. Thank you for bidding.

Sincerely,

Business Administrator to Vendor:

Regarding slow deliveries.

Gentlemen:

The bid award granted you for _____ required that you deliver the initial shipment of _____ to our central supply depot no later than _____.

This date has passed and we have not received delivery. So far as we know there are no unusual events to account for this delay.

We are encountering difficulties in scheduling our _____ _____ operations as a result of this delay.

Please expedite the delayed shipment.

Future avoidable delays in delivery could result in cancellation of this contract and a withdrawal of future bid rights.

Sincerely,

Business Administrator to Vendor:

Complaining about quality of a product.

Gentlemen:

The contract awarded you for _____ contained the following stipulations regarding quality of the product: _____ _____ _____

In using the project we find that it does not meet the stipulations in the following manner: _____ _____ _____

Please contact us immediately regarding this problem.

Thank you.

Sincerely,

Business Administrator to Vendor:

Cancelling contract.

Gentlemen:

The bid award granted you for _____ required that the following conditions be met: _____ _____

You have not met these in spite of our previous letters (copies attached) in which we reminded you of the condition and indicated the possibility of cancellation unless the situation improved.

Improvement has not occurred. Stipulated conditions are still not being met.

We have, therefore, no alternative except to cancel this contract immediately as provided in the bid solicitation and in the bid itself. Payment for that portion of the bid already completed will be made at the next Board meeting.

Cancellation for non-completion means that we will not accept additional bids from your firm for a period of _____ years.

Sincerely,

THE MANAGEMENT FUNCTIONS

The management functions include all those other tasks that fall to the business officer. They include dealings with local public officials when services are needed, with the hospital when employee health examinations are needed, with various school employees regarding payroll deductions, with a seemingly endless variety of jobs.

All of these "other" jobs will require written communications at one time or the other. The business officer should give these the same special care he bestows on the letters involving money.

Letters written to serve these functions tend to have a common content analysis. The following analysis is applicable to all letters concerned with management.

CONTENT ANALYSIS

1. *If possible, especially when dealing with local officials, the letter should be of a confirming nature.*
2. *The letter should deal with a single topic only.*
3. *The letter should state clearly what steps the school district will take in the situation and should detail time schedules and dates.*
4. *The letter should be specific as to what is being requested from the recipient and, again, should state times and dates.*
5. *The letter should indicate any financial considerations as briefly and clearly as possible.*

LETTERS TO MAJOR GOVERNMENTAL AGENCIES

Each year the volume of correspondence increases between school districts and higher levels of government. Increasing also is correspondence with local agencies. These letters involve money, services, cooperative efforts, or concern with legal matters. Not all of this material is routed through the business office, but all of it must be handled carefully. It is important.

Attention to detail becomes acutely critical because of the enormity of the bureaucracy involved, especially at the federal level. Correctness of title of agency is important if speed of delivery is desired; misdirection does cause delays even though the agencies make sincere efforts to route misdirected mail. Reference to the file number assigned by the agency also hastens the reply.

Government agencies are deluged with mail and the harassed functionaries who work in them appreciate clarity and brevity in correspondence. The goal should be a complete, clear, but brief letter, addressed properly, and containing a reference to the required file or control numbers.

LETTERS TO LOCAL GOVERNMENTAL AGENCIES

Local letters should usually be of a confirming nature. Local agencies should be approached in person or by telephone as a matter of courtesy. The confirming letter should be a sort of "minutes of the meeting" and should follow the requirements indicated earlier in this chapter.

Most dealings with local governmental agencies will involve health, safety or police matters due to the nature of a school situation. Good relations with the people in charge of these areas should be cultivated and maintained. Cooperation must be maintained with them and you must remember that cooperation is a two way street: It is difficult to ask the city manager to make special efforts to repair streets around the schools if you have refused to consider letting the school band march in the annual parade.

Business Manager to Chief of Police:

Requesting police coverage.

Dear Chief _____:

This letter is to confirm our conversation held yesterday concerning police coverage for our football games.

We will probably have our usual large crowds at the home games this year and we will need ample coverage by uniformed men. We will have our own teachers on duty in the parking lot, at the gates, and in the stands, but we will need six uniformed men to supplement our people.

We would like the officers to go on duty at 7:00 P.M. and remain until the crowd has left at the close of the game which would be about 11 P.M. As in the past, we will hire your off-duty men for this purpose so as not to cut into the working force and we will pay them the regular departmental scale for such off-duty work. Payment will be made via checks in the week after the game worked.

Attached is a copy of our schedule with the home games marked. We will need coverage for each of these. Please note that all home games this year are at night and on Fridays.

Please send the names of the men and their assigned nights to me as soon as possible.

Thank you for your cooperation.

Sincerely,

You will normally have dealings with other departments of the local government in addition to the police. These agencies should also be approached in person or by phone with a confirming letter following the initial voice approach.

Business Administrator to Highway Supervisor:

Requesting work.

Dear Mr. _____:

As I indicated to you in our conversation yesterday we have a serious problem at the _____ School due to the absence of blinking warning lights to indicate to motorists that they are entering a school zone. For some reason such lights are located on the streets around all of our other schools but not at this site.

The increased traffic on the surrounding streets probably exceeds all of the estimates made when the building was built. However, the traffic is there and so are the children. In our opinion a real danger exists without a warning light.

Would you, please, take steps to install blinking warning lights on the streets around the _____ School. We need these as quickly as we can get them.

Thank you for your help.

Sincerely,

Governmental agencies are not the only ones with whom you may deal. There are institutions such as hospitals and private groups which may impinge upon your office.

For example, cafeteria personnel are required to have yearly physical examinations which include X-rays. Many school districts offer these, as a matter of course, in the local hospital where the facilities, including X-ray and laboratory, are most complete. Arrangements for this should be made by phone with the hospital administration and should be followed with a confirming letter:

Business Administrator to Hospital:

Requesting services.

Dear _____:

This is to confirm our conversation of _____.

The _____ School District desires to have the yearly physical examination of cafeteria workers performed by hospital personnel.

We will bus all of our cafeteria personnel (_____ people) to the hospital at _____ A.M. on _____.

The examinations must include the following: _____
_____
_____

Results of the physical examinations should be sent to Dr. _____, our school physician. The bill for the examination should be sent to the business office.

Thank you for your cooperation.

Sincerely,

Business Administrator to Staff:

Regarding payroll deduction.

These will usually be written in the form of memos from the business manager to all employees of the district or to an entire class of employees, such as all teachers. They should meet all the requirements spelled out in the earlier content analysis.

To: All Professional Employees
From: _____, Business Manager
Subject: Payroll Deduction of Professional Dues
Date: September 1, 19__

The school district will deduct professional dues from the salaries of all professional employees who so desire. We will deduct these monies *only* for those who join the local, state and national associations. The bookkeeping becomes too involved to enable us to deduct dues for those who want to join only one or two of the three associations.

The attached sheet indicates the dues for each association and the total. We will deduct one-twentieth of the total amount from each pay check beginning with that of September 19th and continuing until the total amount is paid.

Any employee who leaves the district before the end of the school year will have any remaining balance for professional dues deducted from his final check. This procedure is necessary since the district will deliver a single check to the local association for all dues to be collected by payroll deduction.

If you desire to have your professional dues collected by payroll deduction, sign the attached sheet and return it to your building principal by September 12th. No one will be granted payroll deduction for dues privileges after that date.

FOOD AND BUS OPERATIONS (THE SPOTLIGHT ITEMS)

Few things in public school work are capable of attracting the attention that comes to the cafeteria and the bus schedule. Though ancillary, these two items are guaranteed to draw the largest crowd at board meetings. Mere mention of a change in bus policy or speculation of an increase in lunch prices will stir up large numbers of citizens who have no other apparent interest in the schools. The same items will also rouse those who do have other interests; they are capable, in fact, of reaching those whose only other school concern lies in winning football games. Because of this widespread interest in busing and food service we believe the business officer should pay special attention to any communications in this area.

Bidding functions, be it buses, tableware, or whatever, should be performed as indicated earlier. Personnel matters likewise would be handled as previously discussed. We are concerned in this section solely with those public communications involving the two spotlight items: buses and cafeterias.

Business Administrator to Parent:

Warning when child misbehaves on bus.

Dear Parent:

As you know we transport large numbers of children to and from school each day. This is a great responsibility for all of us but especially for the drivers who must pilot the buses through rush hour traffic.

Our drivers must devote all of their energies and skills to driving. They must give their undivided attention to the traffic. They cannot act as disciplinarians for the children riding the buses.

We issue reminders like this one to the parents when a child misbehaves on a school bus for the first time. We do this so that the parent can forcefully point out to the child the dangers involved in his conduct. On _____ your son/daughter _____, distracted the driver's attention by _____ _____.

Would you, please, discuss this situation with _____ and impress upon him/her the need for full cooperation on the school bus. Please remind him/her that repetition could result in a suspension of bus riding privileges which would cause great inconvenience for him/her and for you.

Sincerely,

Business Administrator to Parent:

When child is to be deprived of bus privilege.

Dear Parent:

On _____ your son (_____) was disruptive on his school bus. This action was reported to the building principal and was investigated by Mr. _____.

This was not _____'s first disruptive behavior. He has been warned previously that this conduct would not be tolerated. Mr. _____ spoke with you about this problem and warned of a possible withdrawal of bus riding privileges.

Since _____ has continued his disruptive behavior we must withdraw his school bus riding privileges for a period of one week beginning _____. This is in accordance with school board policy (a copy of the policy is attached).

WITHDRAWAL OF BUS RIDING PRIVILEGES DOES NOT RELIEVE THE CHILD OR THE PARENTS OF RESPONSIBILITY UNDER THE SCHOOL ATTENDANCE LAWS. The student must continue to attend school. The parents are required to provide their own transportation while the bus privileges are withdrawn.

Please contact the building principal, Mr. _____, who will discuss this matter with you.

Sincerely,

CONTENT ANALYSIS

1. *The letter states the offense committed and indicates that this is not a first offense.*
2. *The letter indicates that the matter has been investigated by someone higher in authority than the bus driver.*
3. *The letter refers to specific school board policy and attaches a copy of that policy.*
4. *The letter clearly states the period of time and the starting date for withdrawal of bus privileges.*
5. *The letter emphasizes that the parents must now provide transportation for the student since the attendance laws are still applicable.*
6. *The letter requests that the parent contact the principal for further discussion.*

You will have a small number of such cases in any year. Therefore, we think you should avoid a form letter. (Such letters do indicate that there are large numbers of similar cases and you would not want parents to draw this conclusion.) The individually typed pattern letter is appropriate in this case.

There are times, however, when a form letter is desirable. One such time is when a change must be made in bus stops. Another is when a change is to be made in routes, especially if such a change will require walking by students previously bused. In these cases you want to be certain to get your reasoning on the record. News stories in the press and on radio are appropriate; so, too, is a display advertisement in the local paper which should indicate the new schedules in detail. But these are not sufficient. Form letters should be sent to the parents of children involved so that they understand the reasons for the change.

Business Administrator to Parent:

When previously bused students are assigned to walk to school.

Dear Parents:

For the past two years children living in the _____ section and attending the _____ Elementary School have been bused to the school regardless of the distance from home to school. This has been done because of the need to cross Route 413 which is a dangerous road.

Now, however, the Township has built a footbridge over this road at a convenient location. No home in the section is more than ¾ of a mile from the school via the new footbridge. This distance is well within the State prescribed limits at which busing becomes mandatory. (Attached is a copy of school district policy.)

Therefore, we will stop busing _____ Elementary School students residing in the _____ section. The last day for busing of these students will be Friday, _____. After that day, all of these students will become walkers. The start and end of the school day will remain the same.

Thank you for your cooperation.

Sincerely,

CONTENT ANALYSIS

1. The letter states the conditions that justified the previous action.

2. The letter clearly indicates what change in conditions caused the change in busing action.

3. The relevant district policy is included with the letter.

4. The changeover date is stated and there is a direct statement covering any change in the starting or ending time of the school day (if these won't change, say so).

Business Administrator to Parent:

When walkers are to be bused temporarily.

Dear Parent:

Normally students living in the _____ section and attending the _____ Elementary School walk to school since no home in that section is more than ¾ of a mile from the school. This is within the requirements of State law which sets a distance of one mile as the mandatory limit for walkers.

Sometimes conditions require that students living within walking distance be bused temporarily as a matter of safety. Such a condition will be present for the remainder of this school year while the Township installs new sewer lines along Route 413. The open ditches, the stockpiled pipe, the various items of machinery present, all of these will constitute a hazard to children

who must walk in that area. Therefore, beginning Monday, _____
_____, all children living in the _____ section and at-
tending the _____ Elementary School will be bused to and
from school. *This procedure is for the remainder of this school
year only*. Next year the temporary hazard will be gone and these
children will again walk to and from school.

Attached is a copy of the bus schedule for this operation.
Your child will board the bus at the stop indicated on the
schedule.

Any questions on this should be addressed to the building
principal, Mr. _____, who can be reached at _____.

Sincerely,

CONTENT ANALYSIS

1. *There is a specific reference to the previous condition
   with an emphasis on why the students had to walk.*
2. *There is an explanation of the temporary conditions that
   will convert walkers into bused students.*
3. *There is a clear indication of the time limitation along
   with the statement that there will be a reversion to walking status.*
4. *A copy of the bus schedule is enclosed.*
5. *Questions are referred to a specific individual.*

Business Administrator to Parents:

When schedule changes are to be made.

Schedule changes are a fact of life in any transportation system.
They arise on occasion regardless of any amount of planning that may
have gone into the original scheduling. Conditions change; so do
schedules. You can approach bus schedule changes in a positive
manner, treat them as a necessary item, and notify parents before-
hand, or you can approach it in a haphazard, disorganized, non-
communicative manner.

Dear Parent:

Our new junior high school will open when we return to
classes after the Christmas vacation. This relieves a long standing
overcrowded condition at _____ Junior High School.

The junior high school teachers and principals have held
meetings with the students to be transferred. Those students and

their parents have been fully informed of necessary changes in bus schedule and routes.

However, the opening of the new school will require a readjustment of all routes and schedules since we have a limited number of buses. We have tried to stay as close as possible to existing routes and schedules in our revisions and we have had a high degree of success in this. Some changes had to be made.

We have printed completely new schedules and are posting these in every school. We will run an ad listing all schedules in the Evening _____ on December 28th. We are, in addition, enclosing with this letter the bus schedule for the school your child attends. His route and bus stop have been marked in red.

Any questions on this should be addressed to the principal of the building your child attends.

Sincerely,

In addition to points made in previous content analyses, we would stress here the absolute essential that schedule changes must arise from some real need which can be explained to and understood by the parents. State this reason clearly in the letter.

FOOD SERVICES

Many letters regarding food services will be written to suppliers or potential bidders. These should follow the suggestions made earlier in this chapter. Memos or letters covering personnel matters should follow the guidelines offered in Chapter Three. We are concerned, in this section, with those letters which touch on food services to children since these are of prime interest to the parents. Such letters should stick to the facts and should state these briefly. Omit value judgments ("our excellent cafeteria staff . . .").

Business Administrator to Parents:

When cafeteria prices must be raised.

Dear Parent:

For several years now we have maintained a price of 30¢ for the Type A lunch served to children in our school cafeterias. We have held this price even though the actual cost has been higher. Part of the deficit has been made up over the years by the federal subsidies we receive, but the rest of it has been borne by the school district from general funds.

Additional costs are expected next year with the new salary schedules for cafeteria employees and the need to hire more personnel for our new school. These will increase the annual deficit significantly. For this reason the price of the Type A lunch will increase to 35¢ when school reopens next September. This price will, when combined with the federal subsidies, enable us to break even on our cafeteria services provided that the number of meals served remains at approximately the present level. The price of milk served separately, ice cream, and other separate items will remain unchanged.

Thank you for your cooperation.

Sincerely,

Business Administrator to Parents:

Complaint about cafeteria procedures.

Complaints from parents will usually be of an individual nature since the problems from which the complaints arise will usually be of an individual nature. There is one glaring exception to this statement (the forgotten lunch money) and this is covered later in this chapter. We recommend individual letters in almost all complaint cases. These should include the following:

CONTENT ANALYSIS

1. *The parental complaint must be restated briefly at the start of the letter.*
2. *The complaint must be answered directly without evasion.*
3. *The answer should cite general rules if at all possible and should indicate how these apply in the particular case at hand.*
4. *If possible, blame accruing to the child should be minimized.*
5. *Under no circumstances should harsh or unfriendly words be used to the parent.*

Dear Mrs. _____:

This is in response to your letter of January 7th. In that letter you stated that your son purchased an extra pint of milk in the _____ Elementary School cafeteria on January 6th and, after finishing his lunch with its half pint of milk, thought he would be unable to drink the second container. He then, according to your letter, tried to return the unused and unopened carton of milk to the cashier in an attempt to have his nickle refunded. He was told by the cafeteria manager that he could not return the milk. Your letter stated that this was unfair and unreasonable.

I personally investigated the case and I find that you have stated the facts of the case correctly. The child did purchase the additional container of milk and did try to return it for a refund. The container had, apparently, been opened. The cafeteria did refuse to accept the milk for return.

However, the action of the manager was not unreasonable. Her action was, in fact, in keeping with school board policy which is based on health procedures recommended by the State health authorities. Since containers of milk are easily contaminated once removed from the food service area the health authorities recommend that none be accepted for return. Children who do not open their container of milk are urged to take the container home with them.

This procedure is based on school district policy and is followed in all of our schools. (A copy of the policy is enclosed.)

Thank you for writing to us. I do hope this clears up the question you had. Please feel free to contact me if you desire any other information.

Sincerely,

Business Administrator to Parents:

When children forget lunch money.

Children, especially in the elementary schools, will often leave home in the morning without either lunch money or a bag lunch. Schools must provide some lunch for these children but must do so at a price that will not outrage the parents. A simple milk and sandwich approach seems to answer this problem most effectively.

Once the lunch is served, however, there is a matter of collecting the money due. Two procedures are appropriate: (1) The student can be told to bring with him the money due when he comes to school the next day, or (2) a note can be sent home with the child.

We are assuming here that the second option is chosen. We think a form letter along the following lines is in order.

Dear Parent:

Often children forget to bring either money or a bagged lunch to school with them. When that happens we serve the child a lunch of peanut butter and jelly sandwich and a container of milk. We permit the child to bring the modest cost (10¢) to the cafeteria manager on the following school day.

Your child did not have either money or a bagged lunch on _____. He/she was served the peanut butter and jelly sandwich and a container of milk.

Would you, please, send in the 10¢ cost of this lunch with your child when he comes to school tomorrow.

Thank you.

Sincerely,

It would be very difficult to include a sample letter covering each of the nearly countless topics covered by the business department of a school district. We have, therefore, included those we consider to be most common. The guidelines presented in this chapter can, however, be applied to all business letters originating in a school district.

FIVE

"Now Hear This...!"
Effective Internal Communications

The healthy school district, like the healthy body, requires good circulation. Like the body's blood, the school district's accurate and relevant information must circulate to all personnel on all levels in order to maintain the health of the organism

Very few school districts manage to maintain consistently effective lines of communication. Though the problem is both internal and external, for some reason the greatest hardening of informational arteries seems to exist internally, within the district organization itself. When one examines the ludicrous communications problems of our largest districts one is led to an almost inevitable conviction that only a radical decentralization and reorganization of the entire structure could improve anything.

Size alone is not the answer, however. Many small districts suffer from poor communications. Here poor organization, with overlapping lines of authority, is probably the chief culprit.

In our search for villains, we cannot ignore the problem of the person who resists communications. As they say in the Navy, "There's always some so-and-so who doesn't get the word." Then there are those who fail to understand even the clearest communication.

On board Naval ships, every announcement over the public address system is prefaced by three loud, clear words: NOW HEAR THIS. These words are then repeated unless the announcement concerns payday or shore leave. In these two cases "the word" can be whispered once.

This Naval practice has nothing to do with tradition. It merely reflects the communications problem of any large organization. The loud NOW HEAR THIS is what ad men call a "grabber," something to attract attention.

This is not a book about organization. It is a book about communicating by means of effective written messages. In this chapter we will examine the school district's written messages for internal use. Improvements in these can ultimately result in better instruction which is the only reason for the existence of any component of a school district.

ELEMENTS OF GOOD INTERNAL COMMUNICATIONS

The most common form of internal communications (next to the grapevine) is the ubiquitous memo, vastly mishandled, much maligned, yet absolutely essential. Most criteria for good office memos would duplicate those for good letters sent anywhere. There are differences in emphasis, however, for messages which concern the daily routines of the organization, messages which go to people who receive many of them day after day. The following guidelines may be desirable to all written messages, *but they are essential in internal memos.*

1. *The reader's interest must be grasped quickly.* Somehow, by humor, by a startling statement, by an appeal to personal well being or gain, by a threat of consequences, or (at least) by a plea to read on, the message must begin with an equivalent of NOW HEAR THIS.
2. *The message must be as brief as clarity will permit.* Obvious questions must be anticipated, but no attempt should be made to answer every possible question. Curiosity can maintain interest.
3. *The message must go to all concerned.* Better that too many receive a memo than too few; but never adopt the practice of sending everything to everyone.
4. *The message, especially if it is a directive, must answer the six basic questions, who must do what, why, how, where, and when.*

A few years ago one of the authors received a memo from his superintendent which serves as a perfect example of the guidelines offered above. The superintendent had become extremely vexed by a number of new teachers who had failed to submit evidence of their certification despite repeated requests.

Superintendent to Staff:

Memo requesting certification data.

To: All New Teachers in _____
              (NOTE: *It was actually sent to a list of those who had neglected to submit the required forms*)
From: The Superintendent of Schools
Date: _____
Subject: Why You May Receive No Check on Payday

We have requested many times (three times in writing) that you submit to the personnel office your Verification of State Teaching Certificate (Form _____). It is a pale blue slip about 3″ x 5″ in size which you should have received, either upon graduation from a State College or, upon written request, from the Bureau of Certification of the State Department of Education.

Please submit this immediately. By law, we cannot continue to permit you to teach unless we have this certificate. We do not wish to harm our students but we clearly cannot pay you or continue your employment unless we receive your certificate.

Please submit the form to Mrs. _____ in the payroll office. Do so immediately. No paycheck will be issued to you until you have submitted this form.

In this case everyone "got the word," understood it, and complied.

FORMS OF INTERNAL COMMUNICATIONS

"FROM THE DESK OF . . ." NOTEPADS

This common memo form has many advantages. It is easy to use and easy to route. However, it has its disadvantages. It is usually too small for all but the simplest messages. It is usually difficult to make a carbon copy because of the thickness of the paper. In addition, their handiness sometimes tempts hasty actions and hastily written words.

The high school shop teacher, the usual producer of such forms, tends to produce them on excess stock. He should be asked to use lightweight paper, if possible, and to print these pads on paper at least 4″ x 5″. Anything smaller is too limited. The 5″ x 7″ size is fine for folding and stapling.

An ideal use for the small memo pad occurs when one receives a booklet or pamphlet he wishes to share with someone. He can staple or clip a sheet from the pad to the top of the pamphlet with this message (no copy is really needed):

FROM THE DESK OF _____
To: Dr. _____

    I think you would enjoy the middle section on page 14 of this pamphlet. Send it back when you are finished. No hurry.

                                        Signed

COMMERCIAL MEMO PADS

Commercial memo pads solve the copy problem by including either pressure-sensitive second sheets or individual carbon papers between sheets. Some come with different colored second sheets and a few pieces of carbon paper for insertion. They look more professional than the usual school shop products but they are fairly expensive.

Fairly routine matters should be handled by commercial memo pads. Your copy will merely serve to remind you that you did take action.

FROM THE DESK OF _____
To: Mr. _____

    I'd like to see you at your convenience about the meeting you attended at the *Country Squire* on Friday. I understand that Dr. _____ was one of the speakers. Please call Miss _____ for an appointment.

                                        Signed

INDIVIDUALLY TYPED MEMOS

Individually typed memos are subject to all the guidelines indicated for regular letters. They are simply more businesslike and more appropriate for filing as permanent records.

DUPLICATED MEMOS

Duplicated memos are the most common and the most abused type of internal communication in use today. When required, it can be used as a "feedback memo" by leaving space for comments and questions or for an RSVP statement. This is commonly done in notifications of various meetings or for social events. A typical feedback memo might look like this:

WHO?   All Members of the Special Education Staff of the
          _____ Unified School District
WHAT?   Annual Dinner Meeting
WHY?   To plan for next year's meeting schedule and to hear
          _____ of the County Staff discuss "New
          Directions for Special Education as expressed at the
          AASA Convention." _____ is an excep-
          tionally entertaining speaker and he has some truly
          exciting news about the meetings in Atlantic City.
WHERE?   At _____, _____.
          A map is attached.
WHEN?   April 24, 19__ at 7:30 P.M.
          Please clip the bottom portion of this notice and send
it with your check ($5.00 per person) to Mr. _____ be-
fore April 19th.

_____

I shall _____ shall not _____ attend the Special Education Dinner.
I shall bring _____ guests.
                              Signed _____

The following are samples of duplicated memos frequently issued in school districts.

Principal to Teachers:

Procedures for opening day in an elementary school.

To: All Members of the Staff of _____ Elementary
          School
From: _____, Principal
Subject: Here we go again!
Date: _____

What can I say? That summer is nearly over? You are probably beginning to suspect that soon the yellow buses will be rolling and the halls of _____ will be full of laughter, tears, shouting, and learning. That's where you come in, and here is how we will start.

ONE: We all will meet at the _____ High School auditorium on September 2 at 9:00 A.M. for what we hope will be an inspirational address by the Superintendent. He assures me that it will be brief. Coffee will follow along with socialization with old and new friends. You will be amazed at how young the new teachers look.

TWO: We will get together at 11:15 for a brief meeting. I will try to tell you what has happened this summer. You should be happy to see the expanded faculty parking lot!

THREE: After lunch you will be free to work in your rooms. All the supplies you requested should be there. We had to estimate what the new teachers would need. _____ _____, our genial Head Custodian, and I will be in the office to handle your requests until 2:30 P.M. Please let us know what you need. If we don't have it, we will get it.

FOUR: At 4:30 we insist that you join us for a picnic in _____ Park. Let's get acquainted with the new teachers. Your principal will be cooking hot dogs and hamburgers. Complaints will be cheerfully ignored.

Welcome back to _____!

Most teachers face September with positive anticipation. A little cheerful corn in the opening memo can help to sustain the general optimism of opening a new year. There is no need to be subtle, sophisticated, or stuffy.

School opening brings with it numerous problems. Many of these can be eased by the judicious use of memos.

Administration to Teachers:

Testing instructions.

To: All Professional Employees of _____ Junior High School
From: _____, Principal
Subject: Testing Procedures
Date: October 2, 19__

On Monday, October 7th we shall administer the _____ *Verbal Aptitude Test Series, Forms A and B* to all seventh graders. Testing will take place during periods one and two in the Auditorium. Homeroom teachers have been instructed how to divide the students into two segments. The seventh grade segment not being tested during the first period will remain in homeroom while the other segment will report to the Auditorium. The groups will reverse sites during the second period. All eighth and ninth grade students will report to their classes as usual. By period three the entire school will be on the regular schedule.

At the top of this sheet your period assignment and exact duty location for test supervision should be indicated directly under your name. If you have no test assignment, the word "none" should appear under your name. All teachers have been given this instruction sheet whether or not they have a test assignment. The purpose of this is merely to let everyone know what is going on.

If neither an assignment nor the word "none" appears after your name, please check with Mr. _____ in the Guidance office immediately. If a conflict seems to be indicated, check immediately.

Please report to your testing station as promptly as possible. Students are to be seated in chairs upon which lap boards will have been placed. There should be three empty seats between students. Obtain a box of special test pencils from the counselor at the table in front of the Auditorium. Distribute these and the test papers on his instructions. The counselor will direct the students by microphone. Your job is to see that his instructions are carried out. Students will place all their belongings on the floor.

Please watch your area carefully for signs of communication, attempts at peripheral peeking, etc. *Be certain that all students start and stop precisely on orders* from the counselor in charge.

Testing is not the only problem area. Anyone who has worked in a high school will understand the necessity for seemingly harsh controls on the closing housekeeping. Teachers at this time of year are preoccupied with summer plans. Teachers who are leaving the district are not overly concerned with closing formalities. Pity the poor administrator who is filling out a state report in the summer and finds that Miss Smith's attendance data was not turned in. The report must be completed and Miss Smith is touring somewhere in Spain! What can an administrator do? It is far better to keep Miss Smith on the job that last day until she has turned in the needed data.

Principal to Teachers:

Closing school.

To: All Professional Employees Assigned to _____
          High School
From: _____, Principal
Subject: Closing School
Date: June 11, 19__

    You will find detailed instructions concerning each of the following items in your *Teacher's Handbook* which was issued to you in September. If you have misplaced your copy, you may pick one up from the Main Office (see one of the clerks). You must turn in all of the following items before receiving your final paycheck.

1. Make-up tests to be administered where needed or a statement signed by you that none of your students are eligible for summer make-up testing.

2. Your grade book with all marks complete. This will be carefully checked by an administrator.

3. Your attendance summary (Form _____) if you are a homeroom teacher.

4. Your room, desk, and closet keys. Please have them all so that you are not held up when they are checked against your key issue card. This item has been a "bottleneck" in the past. If you have lost a key simply indicate which key on a 3″ x 5″ card and sign your name.

5. Your Release Slip (Form _____) from the librarian indicating that all books have been returned.

A table in the cafeteria will be manned by our two assistant principals and the guidance director from 2:15 to 5:00 P.M. on the last day of school. Simply go to the shortest line and turn in your materials as indicated above. When you have done so, you will receive a receipt. Take this to the main office and one of the clerks will give you your check.

School closing is one problem, graduation another.

Graduation can be a high school principal's major headache. He must issue a series of memos to students, to teachers, to parents. The nature of these memos will depend upon local customs and procedures. One sample will suffice.

Principal to Parents:

Graduation instructions.

To: Parents of Our Graduating Seniors
From: _____, Principal
Subject: Graduation Procedures
Date: June 4, 19__

Congratulations on your efforts, your encouragement, and your patience which will be rewarded on Wednesday evening, June ___th when we will hold our fifty-second graduation ceremony at 6:00 P.M. in the Football Stadium.

In case of rain, the ceremony will be postponed until the same time on Thursday, June ___th at the _____ Hockey Arena on _____ Street at _____ Avenue. Please listen to the hourly newscasts on _____ in case of threatening skies.

There are no reserved seats except those for the faculty who will sit together as a part of the ceremony. I recommend that you try to arrive before 5:30 if you wish to have your choice of seating.

Because of the large number of graduates, we ask your cooperation in the following details:

1. *Please* do not send flowers to the Stadium or the Hockey Arena. We have neither the facilities nor staff to handle them.

2. Do not come onto the field to take pictures. The principal and the superintendent will remain after the ceremonies as long as necessary if you want to photograph your graduate officially receiving his diploma.

3. Please hold your applause until the entire class has received diplomas.

4. Please remind your graduate to hang up his gown as soon as he receives it and to report to the baseball field outside the Stadium at 5:00 to line up for the processional. In case we use the Arena, the class will line up in the west corridor.

5. Please remind your graduate to turn in his cap and gown at the Main Office of the High School any time on the day after graduation. His deposit will be returned at that time. He may keep the tassel for a souvenir.

I shall be looking forward to seeing you at the ceremonies. Thank you for your cooperation.

Graduation, of course, is not the sole crisis faced by principals. Sometimes a major or minor crisis can be prevented by a timely memo.

Principal to Teachers:

Snowball season.

To: All Members of the Staff of _____ Memorial Elementary School
From: _____, Principal
Subject: It's going to snow soon. Snow means snowballs. Snowballs can mean headaches.
Date: _____

The weatherman is threatening us with snow sometime this week. Please refer to page 6 of your *Teacher's Manual* (snowball regulations) and go over these thoroughly with your students as soon as possible. Last year we had one broken window, three black eyes and a bucket of tears. It is time for that ounce of prevention.

Frequent reminders must be issued on various disciplinary procedures.

Principal to Teacher:

Discipline referral procedure.

To: All Professional Employees Assigned to _____ High School
From: _____, Principal
Subject: Referral of Students to Administrators for Disciplinary Action
Date: _____

There seems to be some misunderstanding on the part of a few teachers about what happens when a student is referred to the administration for discipline. I shall attempt to clarify our approach to this matter.

Teachers should usually handle their own discipline problems, including necessary punishment. At times, because of the seriousness of the offense or for a variety of other reasons, the teacher prefers to refer the student to an administrator.

The administrator will await the teacher's report before taking action. Then, however, the referral is total. The disposition of the case will be made on the professional judgment of the administrator, not the teacher. The teacher may recommend action, but the decision will be made by the administrator who is not merely an executioner or an avenging angel. The administrator's decision will be based on *the total school record of the student,* not his record in a given teacher's class. What may appear to be a minor offense to a given teacher may be considered more serious when viewed by an administrator examining the total pattern. And vice versa.

The teacher may request to know what happened, but the administrator cannot seek out each referring teacher in cases of this type. If the teacher is dissatisfied with the results, he should discuss this with the administrator who handled the case. If the teacher is still dissatisfied after this decision, he should appeal the matter to me.

Teachers are often eager to request new textbooks after they have attended a convention and listened to a slick sales pitch.

Superintendent of Schools:

Adoption procedures for new textbooks.

To: All Professional Employees
From: The Superintendent of Schools
Subject: Adoption Procedures for New Textbooks
Date: _____

Textbook adoption procedures are outlined in our Policy Manual, Vol. I, p. _____, Policy _____. I would like to remind all teachers of a few points in the procedure.

1. Any teacher may recommend a new textbook to the Curriculum Council of the District. The recommendation must offer good cause; it should be as complete as possible. It should include a statement indicating specific advantages of the recommended book over the one we now use.

2. Under State Law, a textbook must be in use for at least five years before being replaced unless a significant reason for change (such as important errors in fact, etc.) can be presented to the State Department of Education. Please bear this in mind.

3. New adoptions must be approved by the Curriculum Council and the Superintendent before admission to the School Board for formal adoption.

The stress on memos in this chapter should not be construed to mean that no other communication form has value internally. Obviously, letters can and should be used on numerous occasions when dealing with matters inside the organization. So should personal contact and all other communicative means. Our point here is that the memo is universally used, perhaps overused. By its universality, by its commonality, it tends to be taken for granted.

Our plea is to stop taking the memo for granted. Use it effectively.

SIX

The Administrator's
Letters to Parents

The spoken word has limitations in dealing with parents when the matter concerns their children. Too often they hear what they want to hear. A letter cannot be edited selectively, nor can it be subjected to a selective memory unless it is destroyed. Even then the school still has the carbon copy. Each letter to a parent must be drafted with care precisely because it is a permanent record.

Errors may appear when you send out ten newsletters a year. These can be corrected in subsequent newsletters. But no errors can be tolerated in letters to parents concerning problems of their children. The wording must be simple and clear to avoid the possibility of misinterpretation. The same is true of letters of praise or congratulations for the achievements of a child. When achievement is exaggerated in the letter, you may almost be certain that it will be further elaborated by the parent, resulting in great overstatement which will tend to spoil the child or, more likely, create a credibility gap between the generations.

Letters which carry bad news should, *if at all possible,* be preceded by a personal contact by telephone. This is impossible, of course, for something as common as a routine failing grade, but it must be *made* possible for the student whose failure now precludes the possibility of graduation. When school personnel try but fail to contact parents, this should be noted in the verifying letter.

We recently visited a school district which made no effort at personal parent contact before suspension. Their practice was to send the child home immediately and to mail an explanatory letter to parents sometime during the day.

The time came for a routine suspension of a boy for fighting in the halls. The school sent him home immediately without notice and mailed a form letter to the parents that afternoon. The boy hitched a ride with a driver who became involved in a collision. The boy suffered minor injuries and major fright. The boy's father marched into the school, filled with justifiable fury.

The principal was correct in assigning suspension, but the parent created a public scene because of the evident callous disregard by the administration for the safety of the child. The procedure, needless to say, has been changed. Now the school calls the home, requesting that someone pick up the suspended child at school. Failing this, the student sits in the anteroom until regular dismissal time.

A determination that bad news require an effort at contact before sending the child home could possibly have prevented the preceding difficulty. At a minimum it would have given the school a firmer base upon which to stand. An additional determination not to send any child to an empty home for any reason before the regular close of the school day would have made the school's case impregnable.

We recommend adoption of the procedures indicated in the preceding paragraph. We also recommend that a written notice be sent to the parent in addition to the personal contact: This is the vital record that is not subject to human recall of who said what.

Generally all letters of this type should have the following qualities:

CONTENT ANALYSIS

1. *State the facts of the student's conduct in simple, unemotional prose;*
2. *Include the names of teachers or other personnel whose judgment was involved in decision making;*
3. *Refer to the specific school policy or procedure (or to state law) which covers the offense;*
4. *State the penalty incurred;*
5. *Indicate what steps the parent and the child must take to correct the situation;*

6. *State relevant time limits;*
7. *Indicate the school person with whom contact must be made.*

THE DISCIPLINARIAN'S LETTER
TO PARENTS

In elementary schools, discipline is usually handled by the teachers and/or the principal. This is also true in smaller secondary schools, but in larger schools it should become the responsibility of a team of administrators and specialists. Too often it becomes the total job of one person who is designated as Dean or as assistant principal.

No matter who attends to it, considerable correspondence is involved in this task. To streamline this unpleasant and time consuming task, we recommend a sequence of steps to ease the paperwork load.

The initial step is to maintain a *simple* discipline file consisting of 4″ by 9½″ standard manila envelopes, sturdy enough to withstand constant wear in the cases of frequent offenders. Any envelope size may be used but the size recommended above will serve adequately for almost all of the cases filed. The others can spill over into two or more envelopes which may be held together by elastic bands.

The full name of the student should be printed in a standard place at the top of the envelope with the last name first for alphabetization by grade level. An envelope is initiated on the student's first referral. Thus, only students with discipline referrals will appear in this file. Filing folders could be used, of course, but loose papers of various sizes can best be kept where they belong—in envelopes.

This procedure is not a substitute for the student's cumulative folder which the disciplinarian must also use, especially for chronic problem cases or serious offenses. Carbon copies of letters to parents should be placed in the cumulative folder *and* the discipline envelope.

The great advantage of a discipline file of this type is that it can accommodate all kinds of written material which can, when necessary, be sorted out for summary in the form of a report to a Juvenile Court or a report to the Chief Administrator and the Board of Education if long term suspension becomes necessary.

Teachers should be encouraged to use a referral card designed to fit easily into the discipline envelopes.

DISCIPLINE REFERRAL FORM

Student _____ Teacher _____
Date of Offense _____ Time _____ Place _____
Brief description of incident:

Is this the first offense?   Yes _____   No _____
If YES describe previous action taken by you.
   (use other side)   Signed _____

The referral card, containing all relevant information, should be sent in as soon after the offense as possible but it should not be filled out during class time. It is important that teachers know that they may use any available paper if no cards are available. Red tape must not prevent a report from being written while the incident is fresh in the teacher's mind. Even a one day delay can obscure the facts.

The student should be interviewed by appointment *after* the teacher's report gets to the disciplinarian. In that way the student's version can be assessed after a cooling off period and after a reading of the teacher's report.

When the teacher refers a discipline case to an administrator, he also refers the judgment as to disposition. The discipline administrator is not an executioner. He assigns treatment or punishment based *on the total school record of the student,* not on the behavior pattern in a specific class.

The discipline administrator may not wish to inform every teacher about the disposition of every case unless a specific request is made for the information. If he does wish to report automatically the disposition of each case (rather than simply recording it on the back of a referral card for his own file) the disciplinarian should use a form to simplify the process. The form should be printed on normal paper (rather than a card or heavy paper) so that a carbon copy can be made when it is used. This form and the referral form can be printed in a tear-off pad. In that way the teacher can retain a carbon copy of her referrals.

DISCIPLINE DISPOSITION REPORT

To: _____
From: _____
Subj: Your referral of _____ on (date) _____.
_____ met with student on _____
The following action was taken:

Signed _____

Blank space (with or without lines) is better than a check list because the administration may want to record any number of items such as:

"Letter sent to parents."
"Parent conference requested."
"His adult brother was notified. He seems to be more effective than the parents."
"He seems to be improving in his other classes. See me at your convenience."
"Suspension doesn't work with this one. He wants to be suspended."

These in-house forms are essential to the record keeping phase of school discipline. Teachers and administrators must be aware of their use and must exercise care in filling them out. As we noted earlier these things have a habit of cropping up at later dates. The referral form, for example, might well be shown to parents at a conference.

Normally, these internal forms will be used only by teachers and administrators. Communications from the disciplinarian to the parent will be on form letters for common offenses and by personal letters for more serious offenses. All letters should follow the content analysis indicated earlier in this chapter.

Duplicated forms containing individual policies and procedures affecting students should be available for mailing to parents. Separate sheets should be prepared to cover such aspects as truancy, smoking, detention, cheating, use of cars, bus behavior, etc.

STUDENT DETENTION

One of the oldest practices in American schools is the policy of annoying annoyers by keeping them after school. Although not widely used in our school because we recognize its limitations, it still has the great advantage of being a form of minor punishment that students easily understand.

DETENTION PROCEDURES

Our rules for detention are simple:

1. If a student is not in his seat 5 minutes after the close of school, he is not permitted to complete his detention assignment. Thus, he is referred to the assistant principal for cutting the extra class.
2. Bus students may have a 24 hour delay if they wish in order to arrange transportation. Beyond that time, busing does not excuse a student from detention.
3. Students who work after school may have up to 48 hours to arrange matters with their employers. Beyond that time, work does not excuse a student from detention.
4. If a student wishes to see a teacher after school for special assistance, this takes priority over but does not substitute for detention. The helping teacher must write a note for the student to give to the assistant principal verifying the extra help session. Detention then is postponed for an appropriate period.
5. Students who ride buses to school and students who work or participate in sports after school can avoid detention by simply obeying the rules. A recent study showed that over 85 percent of our students have never received a detention assignment in their entire high school careers.

CLOTHING AND HAIRCUTS

Teachers and administrators should not consider themselves judges of teen-age fashions in hair or dress. We do not insist that students dress as we do.

School people do, however, take seriously their responsibility to educate students and prepare them all for the highest possible achievements. We cannot do this effectively when outlandish clothing and hair styles attract so much attention that learning and teaching take second place.

When a student goes so far with his or her clothing or hair style that it interferes with learning, that student should be asked to make appropriate changes. If cooperation is refused, then parents should be requested to confer with the assistant principal.

No specific standards are needed beyond those of decency, cleanliness, good grooming, and non-interference with teaching and learning. Only the teacher can judge the last item, and the administration must support the opinion of the teacher unless it is obviously unrealistic in terms of the general judgments of the total staff.

Administrator to Parent on Discipline:

Letter for minor violation.

Dear Parent:

Your son/daughter, _____, has been referred to the discipline office due to misconduct.

The specific offense was _____

_____

_____.

He/She must serve _____ days in detention as a result of this misconduct. This penalty is served under my personal supervision each afternoon beginning at _____ P.M. and ending at _____ P.M.

I have spoken with _____ and, after consideration of his/her personal needs and interests, have informed him that this punishment must begin on _____.

We ask that you speak with him/her in order to add your voice to ours in an attempt to prevent any further offenses which might require stronger action.

Please contact me if you have any questions about this.

Thank you for your cooperation.

Sincerely,

Administrator to Parent on Discipline:

Letter for serious offense.

Dear Parent:

Your son/daughter, _____, has been referred to the discipline office for smoking in the school building. The offense occurred at _____ $\frac{\text{A.M.}}{\text{P.M.}}$ on _____.

As you know, this is not _____'s first violation of the smoking regulations. I spoke to you on _____, the time of _____'s first smoking offense, and said then that we would permit him/her to remain in school with a warning but that we would not permit any repetition of this conduct.

Under existing School District policy and regulations, a copy of which are enclosed with this letter, we must suspend _____ for _____ day(s). We require that one or both of the parents accompany the student on the day he/she returns to school after a suspension. Readmission is dependent upon the results of a conference involving the student, the parents, and school personnel.

Please phone my office to arrange for such a conference.

Thank you for your cooperation.

Sincerely,

SCHOOL POLICY REGARDING SMOKING

The _____ School Board passed the following motion at the regular meeting held on _____. As a result, the following is official policy applicable uniformly in all of the District's schools.

SMOKING IN SCHOOL BUILDINGS

In light of existing fire regulations and of health warnings issued by the Surgeon General of the United States, the following will be in effect in all schools in the District:

1. No regularly enrolled student will be permitted to smoke in or on any of our buildings, grounds, or buses at any time.
2. Adults may smoke only in those areas officially designated as smoking areas by the Fire Marshal. These include administrative offices, departmental offices, and faculty dining areas.
3. The superintendent shall draft and distribute regulations designed to implement this policy.

REGULATION

School Board Policy #_____ expressly forbids student smoking at any time in or on any school property.

Building principals will enforce this policy uniformly in all buildings. The principal will take such steps as are needed to prevent smoking, especially in buildings.

The first such offense by any student falls within the principal's discretionary power. The type and length of punishment *short of suspension* is a decision made at the principal's discretion. However, the parents must be notified that the student has violated school policy.

The second such offense by any student *must* result in a suspension from classes with a required conference between one or both of the child's parents and one of the school's administrative officers as a prelude to readmission.

Additional smoking offenses by any student are to be treated as deliberate defiance of school authority.

INFORMATION LETTERS

Most of the disciplinarian's general information to parents can be handled by the type of duplicated policy forms described above. Sometimes, however, there is a need for weekly or bi-weekly reports so that the parent can keep a closer watch on the problem child. This needed information can be obtained on a simple form which each teacher can fill out in a few minutes.

Disciplinarian to Teacher:

Requesting data on student's progress and behavior.

To _____ Date _____
From: Dean of Boys
Subject: Weekly Report on _____

Please fill in the following form by check marks or brief comments and return it to my office before 4 P.M. Friday.

How many absences this week? _____
Is he getting to class on time? Yes _____ No _____
Comment _____
Does he have his books and materials with him?
        Yes _____ No _____
Comment _____
Is he completing assignments? Yes _____ No _____
Comment _____

Is he attentive in class? Yes _____ No _____

Comment _____

Does he contribute to discussions? Yes _____ No _____

Comment _____

Grades Received   Project Work _____

                           Daily Quizzes _____

                           Unit Tests _____

                           Other _____

Describe briefly his attitude _____

_____

                                  _____
                                       (Teacher's Signature)

Photo duplicates of these replies should be made. The disciplinarian should send copies to the parents and file the originals. If, however, a teacher displays poor judgment in the comments or includes confidential information, a paraphrased version must be sent to the parents. This editing should not take much time. Even a large school does not usually have many of these operations going on at a given time. In no case should this procedure continue for more than 3–4 weeks. Continued success or failure will call for other measures.

CONGRATULATORY LETTERS

So much bad news originates in the disciplinarian's office that his congratulatory correspondence should come as a welcome relief. Even though he may duplicate the letters of others, he should send an appropriate form letter or individual letter whenever one of his clients shows appreciable improvement or accomplishes something worthwhile. Often this happens after graduation. All the more reason for a letter of congratulations!

Disciplinarian to Parent:

Improvement of student's behavior.

Dear _____:

My chief responsibility is to encourage considerate individual behavior in a democratic school. Too often this requires reprimands and punishment.

My greatest reward is to see an improvement in the attitude

and behavior of an individual student. This happens often enough so that we cannot write personal letters in every case but I do want to notify the parents when it does occur.

I, therefore, apologize for this form letter, but I do want you to know that ——————— has improved recently as follows:

_____

_____

_____

Please encourage him/her to keep up the good work.

Sincerely,

In the spaces indicated, describe briefly the improvement, such as, "He has not been reported late for classes in three weeks."

Disciplinarian to Parent:

Significant achievement of former behavior problem.

Dear ———————:

I was pleased to read in the ——————— that John has been promoted to Sergeant in the Marine Corps. Could you send me his address so that I can drop him a line?

We had our problems when he was a student, but I knew that he could succeed if he wanted to.

Congratulations to John, and to you.

Sincerely,

A similar letter should, of course, be sent to John.

CONTENT ANALYSIS

Congratulatory letters should be sent, when possible, to the parents of any child who has been involved with the disciplinarian. These letters should contain the following:

1. Some significant achievment spelled out in terms specific enough to indicate that this is an achievement for the student involved (this could be a change in previous behavior patterns);

2. An indication of your pleasure at the achievement;

3. An indication that you knew he could do it all along if only he tried;

*4. A commendation for the parents if they played any part,
   however insignificant, in the achievement;*
5. A statement that even better results are anticipated.

THE PRINCIPAL'S LETTERS TO PARENTS

Principals must also mail letters to parents. Sometimes these will supplement or reinforce those mailed by the disciplinarian. On other occasions, however, the principal will be writing to a student officially unknown to the discipline office. Such notes from principals will usually be congratulatory but not always.

Letters from the principal, be they congratulatory or of a warning nature, should follow the patterns presented in the previous content analyses.

The building principal should try to send congratulatory letters to all students who achieve something outstanding. The particular events considered meritorious will vary with the location of the school. Admission to college might rate such a letter in an inner city school while being treated as a matter of course in a suburban school. The principal must make his choice of what merits a congratulatory letter from him. Once made, though, the decision must be followed religiously—nothing is worse than an inconsistent policy of congratulations.

Principal to Parent:

Significant achievement of student.

It does not matter if similar messages are sent by teachers or others.

Dear _____:

I was delighted to hear that your son, _____, received an appointment to the Naval Academy. He has worked hard to earn this honor and I am certain that he will be an outstanding representative of our school at Annapolis.

My congratulations to you for providing the support and encouragement which helped to make this achievement possible.

Sincerely,

Principal to Student:

Significant achievement.

Dear _____ :

My heartiest congratulations on your appointment to the Naval Academy. I know how hard you worked for this honor and you can be certain that all of us are very proud of you.

Sincerely,

Principal to Parents
of Students Selected for the National Honor Society.

Dear _____ :

Congratulations to you on _____'s selection to the National Honor Society. We know that honors of this type should justly be shared by the parents who provided the encouragement and the discipline necessary for scholastic achievement and character building.

As you know, this award represents more than academic success. Students are also evaluated for their school citizenship, their high ideals, and their moral integrity.

Again, congratulations.

Sincerely,

Principal to Parent:

Significant improvement of student.

Dear _____ :

It is a pleasure to inform you that _____'s attitude toward school has improved greatly in the past few weeks.

His teachers tell me that he is sincerely trying to succeed in all his classes. He is also doing a fine job on the Cross Country team.

Please encourage him to keep up the good work but do not expect too much in the way of improved marks on his next report card. He lost a great deal of time early in the year.

If he continues trying to improve, better marks should appear on the January report.

Sincerely,

In minor matters the district should work out a letter sending system that eliminates duplication. So many variations are possible, however, that we are loath to offer guidelines. Districts would vary practices according to size, according to feelings of administrators and teachers, and even according to availability of funds for postage and stationery.

Such common matters as certificates of appreciation for significant volunteer efforts by citizens for the schools should be prepared in the central office for use by teachers. Failing this, the principal should prepare them in his school. When possible letters should be sent along with the certificates. A regard for the principal's personal public relations might cause his signature to appear on each one, along with that of the issuing teacher.

Member of School Staff to Volunteer:

   With gratitude.

Dear _____:

Thank you for visiting our art seminar and sharing with us your magnificent collection of Gantner lithographs.

Our students enjoyed the presentation and were especially impressed with your comments on the artist's use of color in landscapes. You have advanced their knowledge of technique and have contributed to their appreciation of lithography.

Thank you very much.

Sincerely,

_____   _____
        Teacher   Principal

Letters thanking volunteers for service to the school should:

1. Be individually typed if at at all possible;
2. Be sent, as a matter of course, to all resource people used in a classroom capacity and to all others who perform some unusual service for the school;
3. Make specific mention of the service performed;
4. Contain some reference to a particular part of the service that was especially worthwhile;
5. State how this helped the students of the school;
6. Say thanks.

WARNING LETTERS

One of the most difficult things for a parent to understand is that his child will not graduate with his class or, at lower levels, that he will not move up to the next higher school with his classmates.

The school must provide ample and clear warnings. This is important enough that it should be done by the principal personally. If the responsibility is delegated in a large school, the warning letters should be individually typed and mailed first class. They should be accompanied by a copy for the parent's signature and a stamped, self-addressed envelope in which to return the signed copy to the school. This material should be kept in a separate file for ready reference. A photocopy should also be inserted in the student's cumulative file for access by his counselor. In short, every precaution should be taken to be certain that the parent understands the situation and *that the school has evidence that the parent was informed.*

Principal to Parent:

> *Regarding conditions of Promotion of Student*
> *to a higher level school.*

Dear ＿＿＿＿＿＿＿:

As you know, ＿＿＿＿＿＿ was promoted from ＿＿＿＿＿ Elementary School to ＿＿＿＿＿ Junior High School on trial this year. We think this move is in his best interests if he works to succeed. We want to be certain that you understand the conditions of his promotion.

If, by the end of the first marking period, it appears that he cannot succeed in his academic work, or if he appears to be too immature for his surroundings, it may be necessary to transfer him back to ＿＿＿＿＿ Elementary School.

A decision of this sort would only be made in consultation with you, with his counselor, and with the school psychologist. Such decision would be based on a careful consideration of what is best for the child in every way.

I shall, of course, confer with you before taking any action.

Sincerely,

Principal to Parent:

Reminding him of conditions of promotion within a school.

Dear _____:

Last year _____ failed two major subjects. It is our policy to move students ahead to the junior class regardless of failure. To become a senior, however, a student must have passed a minimum of twelve major subjects, including three years of English, two of social studies, and three of science and mathematics. He must also have passed *American History.*

Unless _____ makes up his failures by carrying extra courses in his junior year or by attending summer school, he will not become a senior next year and, of course, will not graduate with his present class in June, _____.

I suggest that you keep in close touch with his counselor, Mr. _____. Please sign the enclosed copy of this letter and mail it in the enclosed envelope. We want to be certain that parents are informed of matters as important as this.

Sincerely,

Principal to Parent:

Notifying him of repetition of a level in a nongraded school.

Dear _____:

In _____ Elementary School students proceed through each subject as rapidly or as slowly as their ability permits. Each level represents a ten week period for an "average student." This procedure enables a student to repeat a level without losing a full year in the subject.

_____ has had some difficulty in English this year. His teacher has recommended that he repeat level _____. We think that he can do the work but that he needs to reinforce this level before he moves on.

He will have an opportunity to "catch up" either by moving through higher levels more quickly, by transfer to a higher level when he is ready, or by attending summer school.

Repeating a level in a nongraded school is not necessarily a sign of laziness or lack of ability on the part of the student. Some students learn more slowly than others, *but this does not mean that they do not learn as well as the faster ones.* We want them all to learn well at the pace that suits them in each subject.

Please contact me to discuss this further.

Sincerely,

THE HIGH SCHOOL PRINCIPAL'S SPECIAL CASES

Every principal of a large school has a recurring nightmare in which a student receives a non-deserved diploma on graduation day through some clerical error. Caps and gowns and diplomas arrive long before the final accounting for the student who is walking an academic tightrope. This may mean, for some, participation in graduation rehearsals when they are not certain they will graduate. Lines of communication must be carefully maintained between the school and the parents of these academic tightrope performers.

High School Principal to Parent in September of the Student's Senior Year:

Warning of the possibility of non-graduation.

This letter should go, as early as possible in the school year, to parents of all seniors who must pass *all courses* in order to graduate. In schools which require this of all seniors a different criterion must be used to identify the tightrope walkers. The key is that every possible non-graduate be notified in September.

Dear _____:

I would like to join you in watching _____'s work closely this year. A review of the records indicates that *he must pass every subject he is taking in order to graduate in June.*

I do not doubt that he can do this. I feel that your close cooperation and encouragement can help him a great deal. Please keep in touch with his counselor, Mr. _____.

Please sign and return the copy of this letter in the enclosed envelope so that we can be certain that you are aware of the situation.

Sincerely,

High School Principal to Parent at Mid-Year:

Warning of the possibility of the student not graduating.

Dear _____:

I regret to inform you that _____ may not graduate with his class in June. His record shows that he has failed English for the semester. He will have to work very hard to bring his average up to a passing grade. We sincerely want him to graduate and we shall do everything we can to help him but he is the only one who can provide the efforts that are needed.

I would suggest that you contact his counselor as soon as possible. Please sign and return the enclosed copy of this letter.

Sincerely,

High School Principal to Parent:

Final warning on failure.

By now the parents have had two warnings. They should receive one more before the actual notification of failure:

Dear _____:

As I indicated in my letter of January 5, _____ is having difficulty in English. Unless he passes the unit examination to be given next Friday, he will fail for the year. This would mean that he would not graduate in June.

If he does fail, he may take the course in summer school. If he passes it there, he would be eligible for his diploma in September. I would urge you to encourage him to concentrate his efforts in the next few days to prepare for the English examination.

Sincerely,

High School Principal to Parents:

Notifying them that the student will not graduate.

Dear _____:

I regret to inform you that _____ will not graduate with his class on June _____. As I indicated in a letter to you on September 14, he required passing grades in all subjects in order to graduate.

On January 5 and on May 3, I wrote you concerning his difficulties in English. Teachers are usually understanding in cases like this, but his marks in English were far too low to justify passing him.

I would suggest strongly that he attend summer school this year so that I may have the pleasure of presenting him with a diploma in September.

Sincerely,

SPECIAL LETTERS FROM PRINCIPALS TO PARENTS

Occasionally there arises an unusual event requiring special action by the school. Such occurrences should be called to the attention of the parents as promptly as possible. This is best done by a letter from the principal to the parents. These can be sent home with the students but, when secondary schools are involved, we must face the reality that many of the letters written will not arrive there. Postage could be a major item in large schools but, if the event is sufficiently serious, this must be considered. Schools can secure low cost mailing privileges as easily as any other non-profit institution, and this does cut costs significantly.

These special events should not be the sort of things one normally prints in a newsletter. Our view is that a special letter is required for serious cases, especially where possible disturbances are involved.

Dear Parents of _____ High School Students:

We rarely write letters to be sent to all parents. However, on occasion, it is necessary that all parents receive some word of school action. Such a time is now.

As you know we have had disturbances in _____ High School in the last few days. We have investigated these thoroughly and we can say absolutely that the incidents are *not* racial in nature although both whites and blacks have been involved. The problem is one between residents of different areas of the community. Significantly, both blacks and whites from the _____ area have been fighting with whites and blacks from the _____ area. The situation, then, is one of area, not race.

We have taken a number of steps to deal with present disturbances and to prevent future outbreaks.

(1) We have identified and suspended from school all those who have taken a leadership role in the disturbances. These students will remain out of school until we are assured that calm has been restored. None of these students will be readmitted until the student and his parents have had a personal meeting with the building principal, Mr. _____.

(2) Each student now suspended for his role in the disturbances will be notified that any further activity of this nature will

result in an expulsion hearing before the Board of Education with all that this implies.

(3) We have assigned a number of additional teachers to the _____ building. These teachers are drawn from other duties, such as guidance, in other schools. This does pose a hardship in those buildings, but we think they are more needed right now in the _____ High School. These teachers will be assigned to hall supervision and other duties designed to be certain that there are no more disturbances. They will be withdrawn from _____ when it seems reasonable to do so.

(4) Our Student Intergroup Education Committee is now meeting with representative students from both troubled areas, and with other students, to try to define the problems that exist. More important, this Committee will make recommendations for change based on their findings and they have been assured, by me, that these recommendations will be fully considered.

(5) The building principal, Mr. _____, and his staff have taken other steps to assure calm, to assure continuation of education, to assure parents of the safety of their children. Mr. _____ will inform all _____ parents of these steps at the meeting mentioned below.

(6) We have *not* called in the police in this matter and we will not call in the police in future incidents if it is at all possible to avoid doing so. We believe these problems should be handled by the school personnel when possible.

There will be a meeting at _____ High School at 8 P.M. on _____. Please attend. We need your help and your support.

Sincerely,

_____, Superintendent

CONTENT ANALYSIS

Special letters to parents must:
1. *Deal with a problem sufficiently serious to warrant such special notification;*
2. *Be brief enough to be read which, generally, means a a single page;*
3. *State the problem succinctly;*
4. *Detail the school response to the problem;*
5. *Indicate a need for parental cooperation.*

THE SUPERINTENDENT'S LETTERS TO PARENTS

The chief school administrator must use many channels in his efforts to inform the public about their schools. However, his direct communications with individual parents should be limited usually to appeals that have passed through the chain of command.

INFORMATION LETTERS

Superintendent to Parent:

    Response to a complaint.

Dear _____:

    I have reviewed your complaint about buses leaving the _____ Elementary School before the scheduled time. I understand that this causes many students to miss the bus.

    I have asked our transportation director to take up this matter with Mr. _____, the principal of _____ School. I would suggest that the most effective way to air a complaint is to go to the person directly concerned with it. In this case, that would be Mr. _____. Going to him directly assures that corrective action can be taken immediately if the complaint is legitimate. A complaint such as yours would seem to be an easy one to correct right at the school.

    Please let me know if you are not satisfied with the action taken.

Very truly yours,

More often than not, the Superintendent will respond with a referral.

Superintendent to Parent:

    Response to a request for information.

Dear _____:

    I have turned your letter requesting information about the *Initial Teaching Alphabet* over to Miss _____, our Director of Elementary Education. I believe she has excellent brochures on this subject which she will send you.

Sincerely,

A copy of this letter will, of course, go to Miss _____.

LETTERS OF CONGRATULATIONS

The superintendent will want to congratulate students and their parents for outstanding achievements. The information needed to write such letters can be obtained by requiring principals to forward copies of letters of this type. Again, the reader is referred to the content analysis previously offered for such letters.

Superintendent to Parent:

Congratulations.

Dear _____:

The principal of _____ Middle School, Mr. _____, has informed me that your daughter _____, has been selected for the all-state youth orchestra.

We are proud of _____ and you are to be congratulated for encouraging her and making possible the fine musical training that she evidently has had.

Sincerely,

LETTERS OF WARNING

A superintendent's letters of warning should be relatively rare. They should concern only the most serious cases.

Superintendent to Parent:

Possible expulsion of student.

Dear _____:

As you know, your son, _____, has been involved in many unpleasant incidents this year at _____ Middle School. The principal has had four conferences with you. I discussed the matter with you on November 8th in my office and pointed out that we cannot continue to endanger the safety of other students by permitting _____ to fight in school. Yesterday he became involved in a fight in the corridor.

The next time he becomes involved in a fight in school, I shall be forced to ask the Board of Education to expel him from school for the remainder of the year. At that point the responsibility for providing him with an education will, by law, become yours. If you cannot place him in a private school, we would have to take steps to have him admitted to the State Industrial School for Boys.

Sincerely,

When a threat such as this becomes necessary, it must be followed up precisely as indicated in the letter.

Thus far, we have concentrated on letters to parents which originate in administrators' offices. A great many letters to parents should proceed directly from counselors and teachers. The next two chapters will cover letters from these points of origin.

◆

SEVEN

The Counselor's Letters

to Parents

In the secondary schools, where teachers and counselors are exposed to a great many students each week, the task of writing to parents can be formidable. This form of communications is, nevertheless, essential.

Generally the guidance counselor is expected to act as a channel of information between teachers and parents. Since he sometimes has a case load of over 300 students, the counselor can rarely write individual letters. Form letters are his bread and butter in the dissemination of information.

INFORMATION AND ACTION LETTERS

Counselor to Parents:

Introducing himself.

Dear Parents:

Welcome to the _____ High School Community. _____ has been designated as one of my students for counseling. We shall be working together until graduation four years from now.

I would prefer to write you an individual letter, but I am also the counselor for 349 other students, so I must use this form letter. I will try to keep you informed about guidance activities through items in the *Principal's Newsletter* which should come to you every month by mail. At other times I will send you information by various methods we use or by individual letters.

If you wish to see me, please call _____, extension _____. The Guidance Department secretary will make an appointment. On routine matters, we would both save time by using the telephone but, on serious questions, I prefer individual conferences. Our policy does not permit giving out test scores or other personal data on students by telephone.

I am enclosing a booklet entitled *Effective Study Habits.* I would appreciate your reading it and discussing it at home. Parents can help high school students in many ways, particularly with the budgeting of time.

Sincerely,

_____

Printed Name under signature

Counselors write to parents on a variety of occasions. Sometimes the news will be good, as in a congratulatory letter sent to the parents of a counselee who has received a major scholarship. On other occasions news will be bad, as in the case of a student who is doing substandard work. Often the news will be of a neutral or mixed sort. In addition, there are many times during the high school years when some sort of general announcement must be mailed to parents. The letters which follow cover these various situations. All have followed a few rules which are summed up in the analysis.

CONTENT ANALYSIS

1. *Counselor letters to parents should rarely exceed one page in length;*
2. *These letters should cover one topic per letter;*
3. *These letters should state the condition which prompts the letter with as little sugar coating as good manners will permit;*
4. *The counselor should offer a course of action for the parents;*
5. *All pertinent attachments should be included.*

Counselor to Parents:

Curriculum choices facing their child.

Most parents know little about the curriculum choices facing their children. Thus they are not in a position to offer intelligent advice to their children because of this lack of knowledge. Here is a case where the school can solve in advance many of its problems by taking some time and effort to work with parents. Effort spent on preparation of a booklet detailing the whys and wherefores of curriculum choices will be amply rewarded by eliminating some of those thorny problems that arise from misunderstanding. These booklets should be sent home to the parents with an accompanying explanatory letter, at the time students first select their curriculum.

Dear Parent:

All ninth graders will soon be asked to make their choices of the academic track they will follow in their high school careers. Each student is asked to choose one of the following:

the business curriculum
the college preparatory curriculum
the general education curriculum
the technical education curriculum

The choice made now is difficult to change in succeeding years. Hence we ask that both parents and students give long and serious thought to the selection to be made. The final decision should be based on the student's ability and interests as well as on his school record to date.

The enclosed booklet describes each curriculum in detail. Requirements, courses to be taken, and job possibilities for graduates are listed for each curriculum.

The Guidance Office is ready to discuss your child's school work and potential with you. We cannot make the decision as to which curriculum your child should follow: that choice is his or hers—and yours. We can help with facts and explanations and we are prepared to do so. Please call Mr. _____ for an appointment if you wish to discuss this important choice that your child must make.

Sincerely,

Counselor to Parent:

On course choice.

Once a child has begun a particular curriculum path his general course schedule is settled. However, he will still have to make individual course choices from time to time, especially in foreign language areas. Parents should receive a routine letter asking their cooperation and help in the selection process. This letter should detail the choices available and ask that a firm selection be made.

Dear Parent:

Your son/daughter, _____, has chosen to follow the college preparatory curriculum in high school.

Most colleges require two years of a modern language for admission. Some will accept a classical language in place of a modern one, but *not all are willing to do this.*

We require each college preparatory student to take at least two years of a foreign language, modern or classical. We offer Latin as the classical language. French, German, Russian, and Spanish are the modern foreign languages we offer.

We suggest that you discuss this requirement with your child in light of his or her future plans. We recommend special attention to the entrance requirements of those colleges in which your student is interested. You should be certain of their language requirements before your son or daughter makes his/her choice. The guidance office is prepared to aid you with factual information on entrance requirements if you need such help. Please feel free to call on us.

Your child's homeroom teacher will distribute Language Preference forms on the last school day in April. These must be returned within a week.

Sincerely,

LANGUAGE PREFERENCE FORMS

Name of Student: _____ Homeroom: _____
Home address: _____ Phone: _____
_____

Please circle the language you wish to take:
      French   German   Latin   Russian   Spanish
Have you checked the entrance requirements of those colleges you might like to attend to see if they will accept this language? YES   NO

_____   _____
       (student signature)   (signature of parent)

Counselor to Parent:

Suggesting tutoring for child.

Not all students do well. Some perform badly for reasons that are not the fault of the school or its staff. Some students do find a particu lar subject difficult to handle unless provided special help. Tutors may be indicated in these cases. If so, the counselor should say so and should offer suggestions. Some schools provide this sort of help to their students:

Dear Parent:

As you know from report cards and from conferences with me, your son/daughter, _____, has had a great deal of difficulty with work in _____.

His/her _____ teacher, Mr. _____, has given _____ special attention in class and has met with him/her several times after school in an effort to help.

Progress, however, has been painfully slow.

I am convinced that _____ needs special tutoring help. When, in the judgment of the school personnel, it is needed, this help is provided at no cost to the parents.

I think _____ should receive tutoring _____ times a week for the immediate future in an effort to help him in _____. This tutoring can be provided after school right in the building by one of the teachers on the staff. I think such help can get _____'s work up where it should be.

Please phone my office to discuss this possibility with me.

Sincerely,

Other districts do not pay for this service but, instead, leave this expense to the parents.

Dear Parent:

Earlier this year I discussed with you _____'s relatively poor work in English. I stressed the major role English plays in the College Board Examinations and in the admission decisions the colleges make. We agreed that both the home and the school would try to make special efforts to help _____ pull up his work.

The report period just ended does not show the sort of improvement we expected.

Because of this, I think we should seriously consider having _____ tutored in English in addition to his regular class. The school district does not provide such tutoring service. Parents are expected to arrange for this themselves; naturally, parents are expected to pay the tutors for their work.

Attached is a list of teachers living near you who are fully certified and capable of tutoring English. All have done such work in the past and have been successful at it so far as we can determine.

I would suggest that _____ should begin to receive this help as soon as possible.

Sincerely,

Inevitably many of your students will reach that point at which college looms on the immediate horizon. Here, again, parents are not necessarily as informed as you are. Many parents did not themselves receive college educations, and they may not be familiar with the processes involved in applications and acceptances. The guidance office can smooth this path with a few simple communications combined with a meeting or two for all parents. There should be, of course, the possibility for individual meetings for those families that feel a need for such.

Counselor to Parent:

Choice of college.

Dear Parent:

Your son/daughter, _____, has reached the mid-point of the junior year, the time at which each student must seriously examine the question of higher education and its place in his or her future.

Your child, as a college prepartory student, has already decided to go on to higher education. Now he/she must begin to narrow the range of college choices to a manageable few to which to apply.

The guidance department would like to help you and your college bound student in this major undertaking. We are prepared to discuss with you and your child the interests, grades, and abilities of the student and the demands made by various colleges upon those students admitted.

We will not make any decisions for you. You and your child must decide upon what college he or she will attend and no one can make that decision for you. We can, however, furnish you with a great deal of factual information which will aid you in the decision making process and we are ready to do just that.

Please call _____'s counselor, Mr. _____, to arrange an appointment if you desire to have such a discussion.

Sincerely,

Counselor to Parents:

Scholarship aid available.

There are literally thousands of scholarships available and many of these go unfilled each year. How many of your students might fill how many of these if only they knew about them? To ask the question is to imply the answer: Put together a scholarship handbook. It can begin in a small way listing those grants known to you and the rest of the staff, and it can expand year by year as your research and efforts discover other scholarships. But start on it now. And send the following letter to parents along with a copy of the booklet.

Dear Parents:

Each year colleges and universities offer scholarships to thousands of students. Some of these are offered on a basis of need, some are athletic in nature, some are for academic excellence regardless of need, some are highly specialized such as those offered to music majors, others are general in nature and available to all, regardless of curriculum.

In short, scholarships are like the students who hold them: they come in all forms and manner.

Parents are rarely in a position to be fully informed on all available scholarship aid. Increasingly, though, there is a need for this information, since the continued rise in college costs makes it more and more difficult for parents to finance that needed higher education for their children.

That's the purpose of the attached booklet. In it, we have presented information on the types of scholarship aid available. We have listed these by categories shown in the Table of Contents and we have used a standard format to present detailed information about each grant.

We have listed all scholarships known to our Guidance Office. It is possible that we have missed some grant known to you. If so, please tell us about it so we can list it in future issues of our scholarship guide.

If you have any questions about scholarship aid, please call your child's counselor.

Sincerely,

Counselor to Parent:

College board scores.

Dear Parent:

Each year our students take the college board examinations with a mixture of hope and fear. These examinations are important because colleges do use their scores as *one* of the factors which help determine admission.

Attached is a form which indicates the score made by your son or daughter. The form offers a brief explanation of the meaning of this score.

We have scheduled a general meeting on _____ at 8 P.M. in the school auditorium. At that time Mr. _____, our pupil personnel director, will discuss in detail the college board examinations and the meaning of the scores. He will also discuss the part these examination scores play in admission decisions. There will be a question period afterward. The guidance department will schedule individual meetings with any parent who so desires, but we ask that you first attend this general session.

Sincerely,

REFERRALS

Unfortunately, not every problem that you face is as pleasant as the one involving getting the right student into the right college. There are other students and their parents must also receive letters on occasion.

Sometimes the school believes that a particular student should receive some psychological testing. If so, the parents should receive written communication before the fact and should be offered a chance to meet with you in advance.

Counselor to Parent:

Need for psychological testing.

Dear Parent:

Your son/daughter, _____, has been referred to my office because of disruptive classroom behavior.

As you know this is not the first such incident this year. Classroom teachers have tried to deal with the problems arising from _____'s behavior and, having failed to do so successfully, have referred him/her to Mr. _____, our assistant principal, for discipline. The usual counseling and other discipline measures seem not to have the desired effect of improving _____'s classroom behavior.

Now he/she has been referred to me to see if I can help _____ change this disruptive behavior. I have met with him/her. We had a lengthy discussion on the sources of the problem.

I find that I need additional information about _____ if I am to help solve the problem. I am referring him/her to Mr. _____, our school psychologist, with the request that an individual IQ test be administered along with some other tests and a personal interview. Mr. _____ will do this testing within the next week or so and will notify me of the results two or three days after completion of the tests. At that time I will phone and ask you to come in to discuss the results with me in an attempt to get at the root of _____'s classroom misconduct.

Our school policy is to be as humane and patient with each pupil as we can be but never to forget that we have a responsibility to all 1500 pupils enrolled. This latter responsibility means that we cannot "turn the other cheek" forever. _____'s conduct has been such that the school will be forced to take some drastic measure if he/she does not change. This really is why he/she was referred to me. We hope that I can work with you to effect the change that must be made in _____ and made soon.

Please call me if you have any questions or if you wish to discuss this further.

Sincerely,

Often a more detailed examination is required. When indicated, it must be sought.

Counselor to Parent:

Need for psychiatric counseling.

To most Americans the word psychiatrist still conjures up visions of insanity. This view is medieval and irrational but it is there and the school must cope with it. There is no useful purpose served by condemning the public as ignorant. Rather the school, when forced to refer a student to this medical specialty, must be certain that a personal meeting between the parent and the counselor be held. The counselor must, at this meeting, explain the need for such help to the parents and he must, in addition, take time to allay all the fears and suspicions the parents have of psychiatrists. The counselor must be certain that the parents understand the need their child has for the service.

A letter should follow such a meeting. The letter's purpose is to confirm a decision made, to get it on record. Under no circumstances should the letter ever precede the personal meeting.

Dear Parent:

This is to confirm our discussion of _____.

At our meeting we outlined to you all the reasons that convince us that your son/daughter, _____, should be examined by a psychiatrist. We discussed general test results, classroom behavior, and the results of tests administered by our school psychologist. Our school physician, Dr. _____, indicated to you that he believes _____ should be examined by a psychiatrist.

It is our opinion that you should ask your family physician to arrange for _____ to visit whichever psychiatrist he believes best suited.

Please let us know which doctor _____ will visit and the date of the initial visit.

If I can be of further help, please call.

Sincerely,

Psychological and psychiatric examinations often disclose that the child needs to be assigned to some kind of a special class (or whatever name you might call it). Here, too, parents tend to be sensitive. They do not always understand that special education teachers are equipped to provide the special care and help needed by the children assigned to those classes. A personal meeting should be held with the parents of any child being assigned to special education. Detailed explanations of the program and the procedures should be offered at these meetings. However, there should still be a written communication after the meeting so that a record will exist to show that the parents were notified.

Counselor to Parent:

Assigning a child to special education.

Dear _____:

This letter is to confirm the conversation we held on _____ _____.

During our meeting our guidance director, Mr. _____, and I went over all of _____'s test scores and school work with you. We examined the evaluations submitted by _____'s teachers and we discussed the problems he/she is having in class.

Mr. _____ and I suggested to you that _____ should be assigned to a special education class where he can receive the specialized help he needs in order to achieve in school. As we explained to you, special education classes have small numbers of students assigned to them. This enables the teacher to provide much more individual help than is possible in regular classes. In addition the special education teachers can call upon all of our specialists for help, and they do so often.

As we indicated in our conference, we periodically re-examine all work and records of all special education students to determine whether it is possible to transfer a student back to regular classes. We make such a transfer when we think the student can perform regular class work at a satisfactory level.

Please feel free to contact me at _____ if you have any other questions. Mr. _____, who will teach _____ in the special education class, will be happy to meet with you. Please call _____ to set up an appointment.

Thank you for meeting with us.

Sincerely,

Counselor to Parent:

Choice of private school.

There are occasions when the school fails completely. Frequently the parent will recognize this and will suggest a private school. If you concur in this suggestion, by all means cooperate as fully as possible in the selection and assignment of the student to such a school.

Dear Parent:

Your request for help in selection of a private school for your son/daughter, _____, has been carefully considered by myself and other members of the guidance department.

We have studied _____'s records, including class performance and test results. We agree with you that the more individual attention possible in a private school might result in a significant improvement in his/her work. We think the possibility is sufficient enough to transfer _____ to a private school.

Several nearby schools seem equipped to help _____ with his/her academic problems. We would suggest that you contact each of the following to explore their costs and admission requirements: (here should be listed three or four possibilities). We think all of those listed are good schools and we believe that _____ can profit by attending any of them.

Please contact us if we can be of any additional help.

Sincerely,

MISCELLANEOUS COUNSELOR LETTERS

All of the letters in this section are ones that must be written at some time or other by all counselors. They seek information or provide it. Each letter is important, and each serves a valuable purpose.

Counselor to College:

Requesting catalog.

There is probably no such thing as too broad a collection of college catalogs. No one can know in advance which schools will attract the interest of all of the students. Any guidance office can make some good bets on a basis of the colleges normally chosen by the students in their school. Catalogs from these schools should be kept absolutely current. You should make special efforts also to be current on catalogs from the nation's prestige schools and from the federal academies to which your Congressmen might appoint one of your students. You should establish a system whereby the catalogs from other schools are updated on some regular schedule. The important thing is to have a current collection that is broad enough to serve the interests of your students and to have these catalogs available for use. A postcard will be adequate.

Dear Sir:

We maintain a current file of catalogs from those colleges and universities in which our students have expressed a high interest in previous years. _____ is one of those schools which attract a significant number of our graduates.

Would you, please, send us two copies of your _____ catalog. These will be available to students in our Guidance Office, and, on a basis of previous experience, we can anticipate that they will have a wide "readership."

Thank you very much.

Sincerely,

Counselor to College Admissions Office

Some form letter needs to be sent along with the materials that must go to the admissions office when a student applies to a college. A variation of the same letter could be used when business firms ask for transcripts and other school records. The sheer number of such usages in any given year mandate that this be a form letter. Individual letters would be an impossible task. Even individually typed pattern letters would pose a herculean labor in most high schools.

Dear _____:

One of our students, _____, has applied for admission to _____ and has asked that we forward supporting data to you.

Enclosed with this letter are the following:

transcript showing all academic work

an Extracurricular Activity Data Sheet which shows those activities in which the student engaged

a Confidential Evaluation completed by all teachers who had the student last year

Our records show that _____ is in the _____ quintile of his class. The general opinion of the faculty is that _____ will be successful in college.

Please contact me if we can be of any further help.

Sincerely,

Counselor to Admission Office:

Detailing special considerations.

Dear _____ :

One of our students, _____, has applied for admission to _____. We sent his transcript and other records to you late last week.

I am writing this letter because I believe his transcript should not be allowed to stand alone. _____'s work in his junior year was rather bad and it included a failure in math. However, this should not prevent his acceptance into college when considered in the context of events that year.

_____'s father was injured in September, 19__ and was out of work for almost the entire year. The family's reduced income and high medical bills made it absolutely necessary that _____ hold almost a full-time job for that entire year. His parents, much to their credit, insisted that he could not drop out of school as he thought he should. Working as many hours as he did seriously interfered with the time and energy he had left over for a difficult college preparatory course. This showed in his grades.

You will note that he made up his math failure in summer school and, more indicative of his ability, his grades in his senior year are back to their accustomed level now that his father is recovered and _____ need no longer work to support the family.

I think these facts should be taken into account when making an admission judgment on _____. Perhaps, in fact, his initiative and loyalty to his family in an emergency might be good cause to judge his application favorable. I hope so.

Sincerely,

CONTENT ANALYSIS

1. *Special case letters should be individually typed and, above all, should be individually composed to cover the specific case;*
2. *Such letters should state the "fact" that the letter will seek to explain and should do this briefly and clearly;*
3. *The explanation should be to the point and should offer some valid reasons for writing a special letter;*
4. *The letter should show that the situation changed once the special conditions were removed or modified;*

5. *The letter should convert the problem to a "selling point"
if at all possible.*

Counselor to Employer

More and more employers are asking schools for records of
former students who are applicants for jobs. This is a good thing.
Certainly it is a vast improvement over those days when employers
took the applicant's word for his high school career. The increase in
requests for information requires that each school make a determination as to what information and how much of it will be released. In
our view the following is a defensible approach:

CONTENT ANALYSIS

1. *An employer is entitled to know whether or not the
applicant did indeed graduate from high school;*
2. *The employer is entitled to know the applicant's general
attendance and punctuality record;*
3. *The employer is entitled to know the general outline of
the applicant's academic record and may, under some
circumstances, be entitled to know specific achievement
levels as, for example, a prospective employer of a receptionist might like to know how she did in her work
experience program where she was required to serve as a
school receptionist;*
4. *The employer is not entitled to know anything at all
about the student's discipline record, health, or other
confidential information the school may have and should
be bluntly informed that no such information is ever
released if he should ask for it.*

A form letter should be developed to transmit whatever information the school has decided to include in its general releases to
employers:

Dear _____:

_____ was a student in _____ High School
from _____ to _____. He/she did not graduate.

While here, his/her attendance was _____, averaging _____ days a year absent. His/her punctuality was
_____. _____ was an _____ student,
achieving a grade point average of _____ out of 4.0.

Sincerely,

Achievement of a specific course, if release of such information is warranted, can be added in a handwritten note by the counselor.

Counselor to Teacher:

Special handling of a pupil.

Letters are rarely required in this situation. However, some written record is needed for the files. A memo is suggested as the best way to handle this situation. This does not preclude a conversation between the counselor and the teacher or teachers involved. Such personal contact should occur so that the counselor can dispel all doubts the teacher might have regarding any special treatment recommended for a particular child.

To: John Jones's teachers
Fr.   _____, guidance office
Re: John's need for special treatment
Date: December 10, 19__

John's family physician has notified us that John has suffered some temporary damage to his hearing as a result of his recent accident. The doctor says that a hearing aid is not practical at this time which means that John will have some difficulty with his hearing for the foreseeable future.

The family has requested that we do whatever we can to try to compensate for this problem.

Would you please change John's seat in your class so that he will be seated in the front of the room. Also, please bear John's hearing problem in mind at all times when giving oral instructions to him.

Thank you.

CONTENT ANALYSIS

1. *Memos asking for special treatment should specify the condition which requires the special treatment;*
2. *Such memos should indicate the reason for the request and this reason should be one that is generally acceptable;*
3. *The person making the request should offer suggestions for specified teacher actions which will result in the special handling.*

Discussion of the letters flowing from guidance counselors to parents leads logically to consideration of those letters which individual teachers should write to parents. This, unfortunately, is the most neglected avenue of home-school communications; it can be the most productive if utilized correctly. The following chapter considers such letters in some detail.

EIGHT

The Teacher's Letters
to Parents

COMMUNICATIONS PROBLEMS

The most universal complaint of teachers in reference to communications with parents is that the parents who need the most information seem to get the least. PTA meetings are not noted for attracting large audiences, nor do they ever seem to attract significant numbers of parents of problem children. Open house programs that are well attended offer little opportunity for in-depth conferences between teachers and parents.

Newsletters are most faithfully read by parents of successful students. Press releases from school are not always printed. When they are, they are buried deep in the newspaper and are often ignored unless they include students' names or cover competitive athletic events. Television and radio programs involving students or educators are often inept and dull invitations to turn the dial or to explore the refrigerator. We must, therefore, turn to direct correspondence as the single most effective way for teachers to exchange information with parents.

PARENTS ARE SELDOM OBJECTIVE ABOUT THEIR CHILDREN

In any communications with parents, educators must remember that people find it difficult to accept unpleasant truths about their own children. The day is past when a parent would automatically ally himself with a teacher when her decision conflicted with the opinions of the child. Most parents want to cooperate—but they want to see the evidence. Most teachers do not consider this unreasonable since they usually feel the same way about their own children.

GUIDELINES FOR CORRESPONDENCE WITH PARENTS

WHO WRITES WHAT LETTERS?

Good educators are busy people, and letters take time. *But we must point out that good letters can also save time.* Each district must work out efficient procedures for parental correspondence.

Everyone concerned should remember that duplication can do little harm as long as the facts and conclusions are consistently presented. Letters on the same subject to a parent from his child's teacher, counselor, and principal are to be preferred to no letter at all. Three may have much more impact than one.

This chapter suggests points of origin for various types of letters. In most cases these could originate in at least two different places. Each school district should work out its own guidelines. Our format is merely suggestive.

SAVE THOSE LETTERS FROM PARENTS

Letters and notes from parents can become important as supportive evidence. Many a principal-parent conference has unearthed forged tardiness and absence excuses in a student's folder. In this day of photocopy machines, the teacher or counselor can copy parents' letters and file them in two or three convenient places.

THE IMPORTANCE OF PROPER FILING

An intelligently organized filing system can save a great deal of time and trouble. Each person must determine what correspondence he needs for rapid reference and what material should be centrally filed for the convenience of others.

In an elementary school, students' cumulative folders containing parental correspondence may be filed (locked) in the teacher's room or in the principal's office by mutual agreement. In a secondary school, this file must be centrally located for the convenience of counselors and administrators.

Each individual can, however, maintain his own letter file of carbon or photo copies of the original material in the master file.

CONTENT ANALYSIS

1. *The writer should always try for a positive and friendly tone, even when writing to parents who pen nasty letters.*
2. *Letters must and can be written in language understandable to the least intelligent parent. Whenever possible, short simple words should be substituted for professional jargon. Most impressive pedagogical terms really describe fairly simple ideas.*
3. *When a decision or a recommendation is presented, supportive data should be included, but not necessarily in detail. Whenever possible, the supportive opinions of two or more professionals should be included.*
4. *In letters about unpleasant matters, try to establish that justice and compassion have been applied.*
5. *When action is recommended, spell it out clearly.*

WHY TEACHER LETTERS?

A letter from a teacher to a parent carries substantial weight. The parent knows that the teacher (especially in elementary school) is familiar with the child. More important, the parent knows that the teacher is in a strategic position to help the child. Yet we must observe that few teachers write letters to parents.

The reason for this neglect of correspondence with parents is simple. Good teachers are swamped with paperwork. It is our view, however, that letters to parents can save the teacher time in later conferences. It is also our view that teachers can cut corners in correspondence by developing form letters. Sending a duplicated description of a new reading program to 30 sets of parents is infinitely less time consuming than describing the same thing orally in 30 conferences. It even has advantages over a single oral presentation at a PTA meeting. What teacher has all her parents in attendance at a given PTA meeting?

There are additional benefits to be gained as a result of periodic letters home: The parents know what is going on and how their child is doing.

THE "HOW" OF TEACHER LETTERS

Much of the common information from the classroom to the home should be conveyed by principals' or superintendents' newsletters. These can be sent home by younger students and mailed at non-profit institutional rates to homes of older students who cannot usually be relied upon to carry such things home.

Teachers should limit themselves to individual letters in unusual cases and to form letters in matters involving an entire class. If the subject is something pleasant, such as a field trip, the letters will get to the homes in efficient good order.

Teacher to Parent:

A new policy or procedure

Dear _____:

This year our school will try a new plan for the improvement of reading. It is really only new to us. It has been used successfully in other school districts for many years. We are adopting the procedure because it has been successful elsewhere and because we think our children will benefit from it.

The plan is really very simple. All students will be grouped for reading by their actual level of skill regardless of grade assignment. As each student progresses in reading skill, he will be moved to the next higher level. This means that your child may have several different reading teachers this year *but he will remain with me most of the time.*

We expect the children to be slightly confused at first by the change. However, we feel that they will quickly begin to like the new method because they will not be bored by material that is too easy or frightened by material that is too hard.

We have planned 36 levels of reading for the entire school. The average child should move from levels one through six in the first grade, seven through twelve in second grade, and so on. We know that children learn at different speeds *but the child who learns more slowly than another does learn just as well.* Please bear this in mind if your child does not seem to move rapidly through the levels. With this plan he can learn just as well, if not just as fast, as others. Your child is now enrolled in level _____.

I would like to ask for your cooperation for two or three weeks while your child is getting adjusted to the new system. If, after this time, you have a question, please call the principal's office to arrange a conference or to leave a message for me to call you after school.

Sincerely,

Teacher to Parent:

   Explaining an existing practice

Dear _____:

Thank you for your inquiry about the manner in which I handle cheating in my classroom.

Teachers know that this happens on occasion and we recognize that it is not a good thing. We believe that cheating should not be permitted or encouraged for a number of reasons, among them the possibility that this can lead to unfortunate character development.

For that reason I have a clear policy covering cheating in my class. I explain this to the children in general terms in the beginning of the school year and I go over it in some detail with any child who does cheat. The intent, of course, is to help the child understand the possible harm he does to himself by cheating.

A copy of my "policy" on this matter is enclosed for your convenience.

If you would like to discuss this with me further, please call the school office (_____) to make an appointment.

Sincerely,

STATEMENT ON CHEATING AND COPYING

Dear Parents:

I explain very carefully to each new class that the student who cheats or copies another student's work is only cheating himself of a chance to learn. I try to make it clear that marks on tests or written work are only important in helping me to know what needs to be taught.

Because this is important to me, I enforce strict rules during tests. A student who breaks any of these rules has a private conference with me. I tell him then what he did wrong. I also tell him that he is now in the same position as if he had not taken the test at all. Now I will have to find another way to see what he does or does not know. This could mean another test on the same material given to him after school.

The emphasis is not on punishment but on the fact that now we must find another way to learn what he needs to know. This can be annoying to both of us and to his parents.

This information sheet is sent to parents so that we can work together for the best interests of all our children.

Sincerely,

Teacher to Parent:

Explaining a new program

Dear Parents:

During the last school year a nongraded, continuous progress program was instituted in three of our elementary schools. Next year it will be started in our school and your children will participate in it.

The basic purpose of the program is to permit children to progress as rapidly as possible without being held back by a formal grade organization. All progress is continuous under this plan. Your child will simply move ahead in each subject according to what he has learned instead of being confined by what is considered appropriate for the grade he is in.

Pupils will be assigned to rooms based on their individual needs in reading. They will change rooms for mathematics instruction only. First year students will be placed in classes based on reading readiness test scores. All others will be placed according to teacher recommendations which will be based on actual test scores and student accomplishments. Later in the year I shall be able to review with each parent my recommendations for your child for next year.

This new program will be completely explained at the next PTA meeting which will be held in our cafeteria on _____ at _____. At that time you will have an opportunity to have your questions answered.

Sincerely,

Teacher to Parents:

   Open House Day

Dear Parents:

    Monday, October 15, has been set as our fall Open House Day. I shall be happy to meet you in Room 23 at the _____ Elementary School between the hours of 8 A.M. and 5 P.M. This day is intended as an opportunity for parents and teachers to meet. It is an opportunity for parents to see the work of their children. Samples of school work will be displayed on each child's desk.

    If you wish to have a personal conference about your child, please make an appointment to see me on another day. With the parents of 31 children coming on Open House Day, there will probably not be time for a proper individual conference.

    I am available all day except at lunch time. We usually have the fewest visitors between 9 A.M. and 12 noon. Our busiest time is usually from 3:30 to 5 P.M. I take my lunch period from 1:30 to 2 P.M. so that more parents who work in the area can come in on their lunch hours.

    I shall be looking forward to meeting you.

                                                     Sincerely,

Teacher to Parent:

   Requesting assistance

Dear Parent:

    As you know the _____ Elementary School places great stress on field trips as a means of helping our students learn as much as possible about the world in which they live. All _____ teachers incorporate many such trips into their lesson plans.

    The sheer number of these field trips does pose some problems for us. We cannot conduct them unless parents cooperate closely.

    One way in which we ask parents to cooperate is in the matter of chaperons. We need at least two mothers to accompany the teacher and the class on each field trip. We try to space our requests so that no one mother is overburdened.

    Our class will be going on a trip on _____ to _____. We will leave from the school at _____ A.M. and will return no later than _____ P.M. We will use a school bus for transportation. Each child, and each adult, will be expected to provide his or her own lunch; the _____ _____ does have a cafeteria which provides modestly priced lunches and we have been assured that we can utilize this facility.

Could you come with us on this trip as one of our chaperons? We do need your help. We have found that most mothers enjoy these trips as much as the children.

Please let me know soon whether or not you can come with us.

Sincerely,

Teacher to Parent:

Requesting permission for student to attend a field trip

Dear _____ :

The attached information sheet describes a field trip which our class plans to take.

If you wish your child to attend this trip, please fill out the form below the dotted line with the date, your child's name, the date of the trip, and your signature. Return the completed form to me as soon as possible.

Sincerely,

. . . .

Date _____

I hereby give my permission for _____ to attend the _____ School Field Trip on _____ . I understand that the trip will be properly supervised.

Signed _____

The above approval slip cannot prevent a lawsuit from being filed in case of accident, but it will prevent most parents from making unreasonable charges. Courts have almost universally absolved schools from responsibility for accidents when reasonable supervision was provided.

Teacher to Parents or Citizen:

Requesting resource assistance

Dear _____ :

I have heard that you recently returned from a trip to Israel and that you have some interesting slides and movies. I wonder if you would be willing to share your experiences with the children in my class.

I have 31 children, most of whom are 11 or 12 years old. Children of this age can usually remain interested in something like this for 20 to 30 minutes. The best time for us would be any school day between 9:30 and 11 A.M. but I realize that this may not be convenient for you.

Please let me know if you can manage to be with us and what time and date is best for you. My home telephone is _____. The school number is _____.

Sincerely,

Teachers generally and understandably do not like to be called at home. The convenience of a home phone call should, however, be extended when a service of this type is being requested.

CONGRATULATORY LETTERS

Teacher to Parent:

Student improvement

Dear _____:

I am happy to tell you that _____ has shown improvement lately as indicated below. We try to inform parents of good news as well as bad news. I am glad to say that we see so much improvement that we have had to use this form letter to save time.

_____
_____
_____
_____

Sincerely,

This type of letter will undoubtedly find its way home if given to a student in an unsealed envelope.

Teacher to Parent:

Special achievement of student

Dear _____:

Mary's performance in the *Musicale* Wednesday evening was excellent. Seldom do we see such a fine achievement in a child of twelve.

I hope that you encourage her to continue her interest in singing and dancing. If at all possible, she should have individual instruction. I suggest that you ask Mr. _____, our music director, for advice on this matter. Many private teachers are simply not prepared to handle a child with unusual talent.

Congratulations,

Teacher to Parent:

Thanks for major assistance

This can be printed in the form of a certificate. Ask your principal to try to prepare these in the high school graphic arts shop. An offset printing job does look better than a mimeographed form. Since these certificates will be used for years, you should take pains in their preparation. Do a good printing job. Somewhere in your district there is probably a teacher or student who can produce fine lettering in India ink. Use this person's talents to help prepare these certificates. The P.R. reward is great.

Using the offset process you can include eye-catching material— a photo of your school, the district seal, etc.—at a surprisingly low cost. The certificate can be worded as follows:

Medium type: _____ Public Schools
Larger type: The _____ School

CERTIFICATE OF APPRECIATION

Small type: for voluntary assistance in promoting the welfare of
our children by:
Tell how here: _____

_____

Date _____   _____

_____   _____

The place at the lower right should be signed by the teacher and the principal. These certificates should not be given for routine efforts such as attending a field trip (a "thank you" note will suffice there). These can be given to the faithful mothers who are always willing to help, to the extra nice crossing guard, to the father who takes time from work to present a prepared talk and to show his slides of Israel, etc.

Teacher to Parent:

Thanks for minor assistance

Dear _____:

Thanks so much for helping us with the field trip last Wednesday. We all appreciated having you with us.

Sincerely,

WARNING LETTERS

Teacher to Parent:

Need for improvement by his child

The teacher may wish to notify the parent between regular reporting periods when a child begins to develop bad habits. The following form is suggested. Additions or deletions may be relevant depending on the situation. Space should be provided at the bottom for individualized comment.

Dear _____:

From time to time children begin to acquire school habits which can lead to more serious problems. I like to notify the parents of this as early as possible so that we can work together for improvement. The problem indicated below is beginning to become serious. I do not feel that punishment is needed yet but I would appreciate your discussing the matter at home to see if we can avoid serious trouble later.

_____
_____
_____
_____

Please return this form to me with your signature so that I may be certain that you have seen it. Include any comments you wish on the back.

Parent's signature

Date
_____

_____

Sincerely,

Warnings of this type should be dated and delivered in a sealed envelope. It is advantageous to enclose an envelope with your name on it for return delivery.

Teacher to Parent:

Urgently needed improvement

Dear _____:

Your son, _____, has continued to neglect his homework in arithmetic. I have tried to help him several times but he seems to feel that he cannot learn decimals.

I know from his record that he is capable of doing this work. Perhaps if you talk with him in an encouraging way, we can overcome this problem together. I feel that punishment or reprimands at this point would do no good. He needs encouragement.

He will be given small amounts of regular homework in arithmetic every day. I will omit other homework for him so that he can concentrate on this area.

Please call me if you have any questions. The school number is _____. Leave your message with the secretary and I will return your call after school.

Thank you for your help.

Sincerely,

The authors feel that we cannot overstress the importance of teacher-parent contact. Next to actual home visitation and individual parent-teacher conferences in the school, letters from teachers to parents are the best single link between the classroom and the home. Every effort should be made by administrators to encourage the strengthening of this indispensable link.

———◆———

NINE

Writing Policies
and Regulations

YOUR DISTRICT'S MIRROR IMAGE

Every school district and every school in America operates within a framework of purposes, procedures, and rules. When all of these are clearly written and well organized into published, looseleaf collections of policies, regulations, and by-laws which are constantly being updated, we have an image of an orderly school district. When policies are positively stated in terms of desirable purposes, we see a dynamic school district. When the regulations are humane and democratic, we see a district where law is the servant rather than the master of the staff.

In recent years there has been an increasingly broad participation of both teachers and administrators in the constant changing of policies and regulations. This reflects the efforts of our schools to serve a rapidly changing society. No administrator can long avoid direct involvement in the process of recommending changes in and the writing of new policies and regulations. The professional leader is expected to serve the policy making function in an advisory or editorial capacity. This duty should be welcomed, even sought, rather than detested and avoided. The resultant policies and their implementing regulations will directly affect the type of schools in which the administrator will serve.

POLICIES, REGULATIONS, BY-LAWS

At least four elements emerge in the study of policies, regulations, and by-laws. Unfortunately, they cannot be neatly segregated in practice. Let us attempt to clarify this by definition and by example.

Policies

Policies are created by a Board of Education, sometimes acting unilaterally, but more often on the recommendation of administration and staff. Ideally, recommendations should flow from the staff, through the superintendent, to the Board. It must be noted that some of our more militant teachers' organizations are beginning to negotiate policy matters directly with their Boards. The latter, however, still hold the legal authority and responsibility for making policy.

A policy should consist of a clearly written statement but it may be an action, recorded in the minutes of a Board meeting, which serves as a precedent for future operations. The best type of policy is a broad statement of purpose which expresses clearly the intent of the Board. It serves as a guideline for administrative decision making. Policies require procedures for the implementation. These should be expressed in regulations which further clarify the required actions. Procedures can be and are quite often spelled out in the policies themselves.

The following is the opening statement of a policy which does contain some procedural statements:

"REIMBURSEMENT FOR GRADUATE STUDY"[1]

The purpose of this budget provision is to encourage our professional employees to gain more knowledge in their respective academic fields in order that the district might offer to our students those enrichment experiences which come from better prepared teachers.

Procedures

A procedure spells out how the Board wishes to have its intent carried out. This may be expressed in the form of a regulation, which can appear in the district's manual, directly after the policy on paper of a different color. The procedure can be fully embodied in the policy statement itself; it can be implied, even partially stated. The policy

---

[1] *Policies, Regulations, By-Laws, School District of Bristol Township, Bristol, Pennsylvania, Policy #4131.31.*

writer must base his decision in this matter on the need for clarity and on the logic of organization.

In the "live" case cited above, procedure appears *both* in the policy and in an appended regulation. The Board's original intent was to have the complete procedure described in the policy statement. Thus, the following appeared after the opening portion cited above:

A sum of $200 per teacher is provided for in the budget for this incentive reimbursement for tuition only. No employee will be eligible to receive more than $200 under this provision in any one year. This will not be considered part of the employee's salary.

Any employee whose salary is computed under the teachers' salary schedule is eligible for this reimbursement.

The courses taken must be in fields consistent with the employee's logical career pattern. Such courses must contribute to the effectiveness of the employee in the judgment of the superintendent. The courses may be taken in the summer or during the school year.

Transcript, catalog course description, and verification of employee participation and costs must be submitted to the Superintendent's Office before payment will be authorized.

This policy is renewable on a year to year basis. The decision concerning its continuation will be made each year at budget time.

There is no doubt that the procedure in this case could have been more properly written into appended regulations. This was later done.

Regulations

How policy will be implemented by the administration and by the staff members is defined in a regulation. One qualitative difference is that broad procedures can be included within the policy statements but specific minor procedures should appear in the form of regulations.

To return to our case study, the statement of purpose clearly indicated that reimbursement was to be made for study "in their respective academic fields." It soon became clear that the district's great need, in the face of a continuing teacher shortage, was, in many cases, to encourage the completion of certification requirements. In most such instances the teacher's deficiency was in method courses rather than in subject courses. A change seemed necessary, at least in the word "academic." Thus, the policy was broadened by the Board to include methods courses.

A question of intent arose when teachers who were resigning applied for reimbursement for courses taken in their final semester in the District and even for work done in the summer session following their resignations. It seemed quite clear, to us, that such work could hardly offer "enrichment experiences" to our pupils since the "enriched" teachers would not be working in our District. Thus, the need for clarifying procedural statement.

This appeared as a regulation:

REIMBURSEMENT FOR GRADUATE STUDY

Reimbursement under this Policy shall be made only when the teacher is granted graduate credit for the course by the institution at which it is taken.

Reimbursement for tuition under this policy will be made in March and September, following completion of the work.

Since the intent of this Policy is clearly to offer enrichment for our pupils through better prepared teachers, payment cannot be made for work taken in the Spring or Summer sessions when the teacher leaves the District before the start of the next school year. Therefore, those who pursue graduate work in the second or Spring semester (or in the summer) will be reimbursed in the following September, providing that they return to the District in September.

By-Laws

Regulations which govern the internal organization and actions of any group are called by-laws. The School Board must have by-laws. Administrative advisory councils at all levels should also have them.

Since the purpose of the by-laws is to facilitate action in an orderly manner, these should be kept at a minimum. They should deal only with larger matters such as what constitutes a quorum, time and place of regular meetings, statements indicating any permissive deviations from *Robert's Rules of Order,* an indication of how vacancies will be filled, etc. By-laws deal only with the actions of an organization, especially at their meetings.

WHO SHOULD MAKE POLICIES?

Policy making is the legal responsibility of the School Board, and, unless the laws are changed, Boards can neither negotiate away nor delegate this responsibility. Neither can a teachers' organization hold veto power over policies.

Partly as a result of the movement toward broader teacher participation in all phases of school activities, a great many policies are being overhauled. Many more are being created to fill changing needs. Few administrators can avoid the tasks of writing or rewriting policy proposals for Board action. Such efforts do not change the legal mandates, however.

WHO SHOULD WRITE POLICIES AND REGULATIONS?

The same person should do all of the writing of policies and regulations in order to maintain consistency of prose. The text produced by this individual should be reviewed by other people or groups and by the chief administrator to be certain that it says what was actually intended. Finally, of course, the draft will be reviewed by the Board. Needed revisions should be made by the original writer. In many cases, particularly in smaller districts, the only person qualified to do the writing would be the superintendent.

WHERE DO YOU START?

No Policy Book?

If, as is true of far too many districts, no single policy book exists, a tremendous task looms ahead. Short-cuts must be taken or the work of establishing the basic manual will drag on for years. Having an existing policy book is of little help if it has not been updated for several years. Good practices change constantly. Attitudes change, problems change. Policies and regulations cannot remain current for long. The creation of a good current policy book, like a journey of a thousand miles, starts with a single step.

What Should Be Your First Step?

The thoroughness that usually attends the beginning of a formidable task might dictate a study of Board minutes for a number of years
back as a preliminary step to the creation of a suitable manual. We
believe that this is a back-breaking and fruitless approach. One of the
authors once spent several days tracing *one policy* (maternity leave)
back through five years of board minutes. He found four mutually
contradictory decisions, two of which violated current state law. He
also found three changes in state law over the same five year period.

We urge a more practical beginning. We think any approach
must include (1) a working knowledge of, and constant reference to,
a current manual of state educational laws, and (2) a sound knowledge of good, accepted practices in the nation's better school districts.
These should then be combined with a knowledge of local needs and
practices which must be considered in policy writing. From this base,
you can proceed to possible short-cuts.

Short-Cut #1 is the most promising if your policies are really in
bad shape. This approach is to engage a consulting firm which special-
izes in this type of work. An administrator should be given responsibility for direct liaison duty with the firm. The Board and staff should
become involved according to the procedures of the firm. Some of the
advantages of this approach are:

1. The job will be finished in a reasonable period of time—one to two
   years.
2. The firm will have the advantage of wide experience with some of
   the best available policies.
3. The firm will probably furnish legal consultation. (It should.)
4. A superior organizational format will result.
5. A sound, up to date, and complete set of policies can be reviewed
   by the Board. After modifications, deletions, and additions, all of
   the contradictory and fuzzy practices of the past can be super-
   ceded at one time, thus greatly simplifying future problems of research.

The only real disadvantage of this approach lies in the fact that
the administrator assigned this responsibility will have to curtail some
of his regular duties during most of the life of the project. The District
should analyze this problem before adopting this course.

A lesser difficulty of working with a consultant is that the outsider has no knowledge of local needs and traditions. This can be overcome by the liaison administrator from the District. It should also be noted that consultants cost money. But the Board cannot expect that a number of staff members can do the same job as the consultant could do in the same period of time without seriously neglecting their normal duties.

Short-Cut #2 is to "free" a full-time administrator by spreading his normal responsibilities among a number of his colleagues and to give him the support of a directing committee. He can then study and borrow from the policy books of many superior school districts. Policies, as such, are not covered by copyright laws and it is customary in American education to share rather liberally our better ideas. Indeed, some dubious ideas are sometimes shared widely by being touted in the professional literature.

There is, nevertheless, some question of ethics here. There might also be a matter of legality involved if you copy substantially a system of classification developed by a consulting firm for use in another district. Furthermore, there is no assurance that the job can be completed this way in a reasonable period of time. Even more time might be taken from district administrative duties by this method than by the first "short-cut" listed above.

Short-Cut #3 consists of hiring a bright young administrative intern with special qualifications in this field (and in writing) and assigning to him this task full-time for a year. This could cost the district about as much as the price of a consulting firm if the necessary clerical assistance is taken into consideration. It would also short-change the intern by depriving him of needed experience in all of the other facets of administration.

Ultimately, of course, whichever route is chosen, some administrators must become involved in the actual writing of policies and procedures.

PATTERNS OF ORGANIZATION

There are many ways to organize and codify policies and regulations. You may choose to develop your own. Most organizational patterns involve from six to nine major headings. Few go beyond ten. These headings must be broad but precise. They must be flexible without being loose. They must provide for comprehensive internal subdivision with letter and number codification that can expand liberally at any given point without confusion.

The best procedure, in the beginning, is to examine carefully several policy systems which have worked well for others over a period of years. Examine the rationale for each. Take a critical look at both advantages and disadvantages of each system. Then you can decide on a modification that best suits your district.

Some examples of major headings in common policy use are:

Board of Education, including its by-laws
  This section is absolutely essential.

Personnel
  This is frequently subdivided into categories for professional and non-professional personnel.

Pupils or Students
  This is also essential.

Business Affairs
  This is sometimes combined with plant construction and maintenance, sometimes with non-professional personnel, and sometimes it exists as a subcategory under *administration.*

Administration
  Again, this is a necessary major heading. If the policy book does one thing, it should provide a clear distinction between, and definitions of, the rights and responsibilities of the *Board of Education* and of the *Administration.*

The Community
  The relationship between the community and its schools is frequently listed as a major heading.

Curriculum or Instruction
  This deserves major consideration.
  Some districts may have continuing problems which require major considerations in policies and regulations. Rapidly growing districts, for example, may need a separate heading for *Construction.* Cities may choose to have one for *Intergroup Relations.* All major headings should be tabbed in the book for ready reference.

POLICY WRITING GUIDELINES

1. Start with a Desirable and Reasonable Goal

"The provision of individualized instruction" cannot be considered a reasonable goal for a public school district. The phrase is just too vague. Meaningless phrases should be avoided by policy writers. They should remain the property of those who write articles for professional journals. Policy writers are expected to produce prose which leads to *action*.

2. State Clearly the Intention of the Policy

"In order to move toward individualization of instruction, the X School District shall provide adequate numbers of specialized supportive teachers.

"This support shall be in the areas of guidance, diagnostic psychological services, social workers for home visitation, reading specialists, audio-visual aid's service, a special education program, programs for gifted students, and adequate library service."

The policy intent is clearer now than it was above but still it is not fully satisfactory.

3. Indicate Broad Implementation

The policy indicated above should now go on to clarify case loads for full-time specialists, the extent of the District's participation in state and county programs and in the programs of other jointures, the involvement of university or private consultants, and similar items.

4. Research Precedents Should Be Indicated

Research in education is often maligned as being trivial and repetitive. But, in its broadest sense, some research is necessary for any policy. Why are we recommending this policy at this time? Why not its opposite? Why any policy at all? There must be some good reason beyond whim or hunch. For example:

> A board member claims that the District has never involved itself in violating the sanctity of the home by having school personnel visit the homes without specific invitations. He insists that social workers are provided by the County Welfare Department, anyhow. He asks: "Why should we become involved?"
>
> Research of Board minutes reveals that, when the truant officer was replaced fifteen years ago, a retired teacher was hired and clearly instructed to visit the homes of problem students as requested by the principals.

Queries of surrounding districts reveal that home visitation is considered a sound practice. One district employs several home visitors under an ESEA Title I grant which indicates governmental approval of the practice.

Research of professional literature reveals that the practice is considered desirable by experts.

A statement summarizing these findings, inserted in the policy before the section on implementation, can forestall future similar questions.

5. Research the Legality of New Policies

The Board Attorney should check all new policy statements to be certain they comply with the law. Obviously, this should be done before the Board adopts the policy.

6. Date Adoptions and Modifications at the Bottom of the Last Page of the Policy

Example:

Adopted:	9/17/59
Modified:	10/12/68

POLICY WRITING PITFALLS TO AVOID

1. Overuse of Technical Expressions

Policy books are written for public use as well as for guidance of professional educators. These manuals are prepared to be read by everyone and anyone—by parents, by novice teachers, by old timers, by board members, and by administrators. They must be comprehensible to all. They will not necessarily be understood by everyone. It is easy to fall into technical usages if one is not careful. The knowledge that the entire book cannot be rewritten every year should mitigate against the use of colloquialisms since these change as often as milady's fashions.

2. Taking Seemingly Obvious Matters for Granted

Nothing causes so many problems as the obvious. Because something is considered obvious it can be interpreted to the satisfaction of any reader. What is meant, for example, when the district prints a salary schedule containing a number of orderly steps? To a teacher it is *obvious* that progression through the steps is automatic, year by year. To the administrator it may be *obvious* that the progression depends upon satisfactory ratings. Why not remove the problem in advance by stating the obvious in clear English at the bottom of the salary schedule?

3. Printing Policies in Permanent Format

Policies should be published in a manner to indicate that they are not the Ten Commandments. They can, and probably will, undergo change. They should be bound in looseleaf fashion. The responsibility for updating policy books periodically should be clearly designated to one person. The superintendent's secretary is often selected for the job which is typically done in the summer when the books lie dormant.

4. Too Narrow Topics

Policy deals with broad aspects of school activities. In the example of supportive services to improve instruction cited above, it would be possible to write a policy for each type of service. This is not recommended precisely because it narrows things far too much.

Administrators often succumb to the lure of having a policy to cover every specific eventuality. Such men try to write a new policy as each new problem arises. We think this is self-defeating since it is almost impossible to anticipate every eventuality and, worse, the mass of policies that result from such efforts form a guardhouse lawyer's delight. It is wiser to concentrate policy efforts on the broad topic while leaving specificity to regulations.

Below is a sample policy from the writers' own district. The regulation which implements it follows the policy.

4115

Personnel　　　　　　　　　　　　　　　　*Policy #4215*
Assignment and Transfer
The superintendent is authorized to assign, reassign, or transfer all professional and non-professional personnel in the best interest of the school district.
Policy
adopted: *9/66*　　　　　　　School District of Bristol Township
　　　　　　　　　　　　　　Bristol, Pennsylvania

Personnel   *Policy #4115R*
Assignment and Transfer

1. *Teacher requested transfers between buildings within the district.*
   a. The teacher desiring a transfer must make his request in writing to the superintendent before April 1 of the school year preceding the transfer.
   b. The teacher must clearly state specific reasons for requesting the transfer. The teacher should designate a building to which he wishes to transfer.
   c. A staff vacancy must exist in the school to which the teacher wishes to transfer for any consideration to be given to the request.
   d. The principal of the "sending school" must be notified of the requested transfer. His recommendation will be considered by the superintendent in making a final decision.
   e. No requests for transfer will be considered from non-tenure teachers.
   f. The request for transfer will be granted if it is not detrimental to the instruction program of the Bristol Township School District.

2. *Transfers not requested by teachers.*
   The superintendent has the right to transfer any personnel of the district, professional or non-professional, when, in his opinion, such transfer is in the best interest of the school district. In such cases every effort will be made, *when possible,* to confer with the employee involved at the earliest possible time. The best interests of the program of instruction will, however, remain the most important criterion in this decision.

Rules   By _____
Approved: _____   Bristol, Pennsylvania

TEN

The Paperwork of

Professional Negotiations

History may well characterize the past decade as the golden age of pressure groups, as a time of fierce mini-revolutions all over the world. Incidents of courageous, sometimes pointless, militancy have ranged from the quixotic students of Prague defying the Soviet Army to American high school students demonstrating for a smoking room. Teachers, too, have caught the urge.

Teacher militancy does not appear destined to run the course of a brush fire. It has been adopted as a way of life by both major teacher organizations. It has paid magnificent dividends. One of its by-products is the adoption from industry of the method of decision making about salaries and working conditions known as collective bargaining. In education, the term used to describe this procedure is *professional negotiations*.

Accurate record keeping and correspondence is a vital part of this process, both for teachers and for boards of education. The writers know of one district in which an entire year of negotiations was obscured because one side insisted that a two-year agreement was in force and the other side was certain that a one-year agreement had been effected. Nobody had taken the trouble to record the length of time of agreement!

The purpose of this chapter is to guide both sides through the tricky paperwork of a typical year of professional negotiations.

PRELIMINARY CORRESPONDENCE

Both sides need to come to the negotiating table with accurate data. Most communities want to offer salaries and working conditions roughly equal to school districts with which they *actually* compete for teachers. Few communities want to take a substantial lead and virtually none is interested in "keeping up with the wealthier Joneses."

This results in a frantic effort to know what is going on in neighboring districts while maintaining some local secrecy. The intrigue involved often parallels that seen in the auto industry when new models are in the early stages of design. Some boards fear to lose their advantage if they share with neighboring boards those secret agreements the members have made among themselves. They fear this will "leak" to teacher negotiations. To permit the team on the opposite side of the table to know how far "our" team will yield is an unforgivable weakness. The result is that the process sometimes assumes the rigid conventions of a classical Japanese drama.

Realistically, however, both sides need two kinds of salary information from neighboring districts: (1) factual data on what firm agreements will be reached and (2) inside information or educated guesses on how far competing districts will go if necessary.

The former is easy to obtain by simple letters of request or through regional or state publications. The latter, obtained with cloak and dagger difficulty, is extremely useful in the strategy conferences of the negotiating teams. The teachers' negotiators hate to lose face by accepting a salary contract lower than that of competing districts. The board fears taxpayer irritation if they come out too far ahead of their neighbors. Both sides, then, have an interest in gathering the information.

Teachers' Negotiators to Other Districts:

Requesting salary data

This letter should go from the president of the teachers' organization to his opposite members in competing districts.

Dear _____:

Enclosed is a copy of our current salary schedule. Please send us a copy of your scale. Do you have any firm data on negotiations progress thus far? We have not yet started formal negotiations.

Sincerely,

The aforementioned cloak and dagger information is often obtained in personal conferences, between teacher-friends who work in different districts. Frequently, however, formal requests for information must be made. In such cases, it is important to spell out the exact data desired.

Teachers' Negotiators to Other Districts:

Requesting information on teaching load

Dear _____:

In our negotiations this year, we are particularly anxious to attack the problem of teaching load in our secondary schools. The attached data sheet covers all facets of our current work load. Could you, please, send us the following data concerning your situation?

1. The average number of conventional academic classes taught by secondary teachers in your district. By this we mean one teacher (not as a team member) teaching a normal class alone and meeting them five times a week for one period each day in English, social studies, foreign languages, mathematics, science, or business education.

2. The average size of the above classes.

3. The average number of classes per week and average student load per week of each of the following categories at the secondary level: industrial arts, art, music, home economics, physical education (per teacher, not per class of 2 or 3 teachers).

4. The average student case load of guidance counselors.

5. The average student case load of work-experience supervisors.

6. A general policy statement on the distribution of supervision duties which receive no extra compensation such as study halls, buses, cafeteria, auditorium, etc.

7. A list of duties which receive extra compensation and the amount allocated to each.

We realize the difficulties involved in correlating the data of different districts but we feel that, if we all get together on this, we may be able to obtain adoption of the best current practices of each district *for all districts*. Please help us.

We will send you a copy of the compilation of data we will make as a result of this request and others like it.

Sincerely,

With minor modifications, the superintendents can obtain similar information from each other for their boards. This, though, is one area in which agreement should be reached: Why duplicate effort? Why not send a single request and share this non-sensitive information?

ESTABLISHING GROUND RULES

Ground rules and meeting dates can be established through correspondence or through preliminary meetings but, in either case, the agreements must be recorded. We think this is best done through correspondence.

School Board to Teachers' Negotiators:

Suggesting ground rules for negotiations

Dear _____:

The Board would like to propose the following procedures for negotiations this year. Please let us know as soon as possible if your group agrees.

1. Regular meetings will be held on Tuesday evenings from 8 to 11 P.M. in the Cafeteria of the Administration Building.
2. The chairmanship of meetings will alternate between the chief negotiators of the Board and of the teachers.
3. Meetings will end at 11 P.M. unless both parties agree to an extension.
4. Extra meetings will be scheduled by mutual consent.
5. Each team may bring in consultants or special witnesses with the consent of the other team. This consent must have been obtained normally at the previous meeting. In unusual circumstances, one chief negotiator may obtain permission from his opposite member by telephone 48 hours or more before the meeting in question. Each team must empower its chief negotiator to grant this permission.

6. One representative from the elementary principals and one from the secondary principals shall be present at every session. It is understood that they shall not participate in discussions concerning the basic teachers' salary schedule but they may be heard on any other matters upon recognition by the chairman.

7. Discussion will be informal but, in cases of disagreement, *Robert's Rules of Order* shall prevail.

Sincerely,

Letters Confirming Representatives and Their Authority:

1. From the teachers

Dear _____:

    The attached list of teachers constitute the teachers' negotiations team for 19__–19__. Mr. _____ has been designated as chairman. The team has been authorized to speak for the teachers on all contractual matters and to make any necessary agreements.

    The team may decide, however, to submit any question to the Teachers' Council or to the entire membership of the association for ratification.

Sincerely,

2. From the board

Dear _____:

    The attached list of Board members and the Superintendent of Schools shall constitute the Negotiations Team for the Board of Education for 19__–19__. The Personnel Director, Mr. _____, shall, with the agreement of the teachers' team, act as secretary for the meetings.

    The Board negotiating team has been granted discretionary authority by the Board but the team must submit to the entire Board decisions which involve additional tax levies.

Sincerely,

Card Reminding All Participants of Meetings

Simple postcards should be sent to all participants three or four days before meetings.

Reminder: Negotiations Meeting
At: _____
Date: _____ *Time:* _____

PROGRESS REPORTS

Both teams may wish to report periodically to the entire staff or
to the public. This, of course, is an opportunity for each group to
present its own version of the story. Highly emotional partisanship can
obscure objectivity, a point that should be weighed by those who
would report these sessions. Assume, for the moment, a set of circumstances leading to an impasse. Each side *might* report this as a
segment of a progress report. Each might produce a report biased in
its own favor. The same data can be written to avoid inflaming
emotions and this is to be preferred.

THE SET OF FACTS

School Board practices have gradually evolved from an administrative function in the early days of the Republic to a policy making
function today. In enlightened districts, the chief administrator involves teachers and administrators in an advisory capacity on matters
of policy. He then *recommends* policy to the Board. The Board hears
the facts and opinions of the staff and the chief administrator. Then
the Board acts *as it sees fit.* In some states the law specifically denies to
the school boards the right to delegate its policy making function to
anyone.

Assume a state which mandates policy making to the Board.
Further assume that the Superintendent of Schools works with a
representative group of teachers and administrators which advises him
on policy matters. During teacher-board negotiations, the teachers
submit the following items to be inserted in a new contract:

> No policy changes affecting teachers' working conditions shall be
> made by the board without consulting the Teachers' Association
> and without the consent of the latter.

The position taken by the Board is that this would, in effect, be a
delegation of its policy making power and that this delegation is
contrary to law.

The teachers argue that an "advisory" group with no power is a futile arrangement and a waste of time. Working conditions are negotiable according to law. Why can the Board circumvent this by a unilateral power to make policy?

An impasse results.

Here are two reports of the above situation as they might be written by angry teachers and by angry administrators who are deeply involved in the situation.

PROGRESS REPORT FROM TEACHERS TO TEACHERS

Negotiation came to a halt last night as the board refused to accept a contractual guarantee of teachers' legal and moral right to negotiate. Your negotiating team feels that this is a fundamental issue which is not taken care of by a *puppet* teachers' advisory committee on policy. What good is our advice when the board can ignore it at will? Where is democracy in our district? We refuse to bow down to dictatorship! Are you with us?

PROGRESS REPORT FROM BOARD TO TEACHERS

Negotiations ceased last night. They will not continue until the teachers' negotiators will accept the simple fact that *the board will not violate the laws of our state* in a contract.

To request *consent* of the Teachers' Association for the passage of a policy is to delegate to the Association the power of policy making.

Art. _____ Bill _____ Ed. passed on September _____, 19__ clearly states:

No school board may delegate its responsibility and authority to make necessary policies regarding any aspect of the operation of its public schools. . . .

The law is clear. The board intends to uphold the law as its members have been sworn to do.

AN OBJECTIVE PROGRESS REPORT

Negotiations progress has been temporarily delayed because of a failure to agree on the wording of a section of the new contract dealing with the participation of teachers in policy making.

Two laws seem to be in conflict. One law gives teachers the right to negotiate working conditions (citation of the appropriate section). The other law specifically denies the board permission to delegate its policy making power (citation of the appropriate section).

The impasse centers on the word "consent" in the proposed contract clause (citation of contract clause).

Both sides will seek legal advice on this matter and attempt to find other words to express more clearly the intent of everyone concerned to provide for democratic participation in a meaningful way within legal restrictions.

(Here would follow the intentions of the group issuing this report.)

The objective report sticks to facts and avoids emotional terms. It is dispassionate. Therein lies its value.

MINUTES OF NEGOTIATIONS MEETINGS

Negotiations meetings between teachers' representatives and board negotiators often assume a rigidly ritualistic structure. Role playing is common as the partisan feelings of teachers and taxpayers are exhibited by their representatives "on stage." All negotiators have some awareness of their responsibilities to their constituents. All must demonstrate their devotion to the role assigned them. It is only fair to record such pronouncements in the minutes. It is not necessary, however, to record these verbatim as is done in the *Congressional Record*.

Most negotiating teams prefer not to have a stenographer present at meetings. A teacher or an administrator selected by mutual consent should record the minutes. The person chosen to do this needs experience and understanding to evaluate the histrionics of negotiations and to record the proceedings intelligently. He must be mature, level headed, and unemotional.

Minutes should include the following:

1. Time, date, place of meeting, and parties present.
2. An accurate statement of the issue under discussion.
3. A brief resume of each viewpoint expressed and the name of the speaker.
4. Failure of agreement items and specific postponement dates for further discussion.
5. An exact statement of agreement. It is good to key agreements in

the format so that they can be spotted quickly by someone scanning a whole year's set of minutes. (See example below.)

6. Date, time, and place of next meeting.
7. Signatures of both chief negotiators attesting to the validity of minutes. These should be obtained *immediately* after the meeting. Differences of opinion on the minutes should be resolved immediately if possible.
8. The signature of the recorder.

SAMPLE MINUTES OF A NEGOTIATION SESSION

Minutes of Negotiation Meeting, September ____, 19__

The meeting, held in the Cafeteria of the _____ School, was called to order at 8:24 P.M. on September ____, 19__. The following were present: *Board Negotiators:* (list by name and position). *Teachers Negotiators:* (list by name and position). *Others:* Recorder of Minutes (list name), (list all others by name and position).

The proposed Article IV, Section 3 was discussed.
No policy changes affecting teachers' working conditions shall be made by the board without consulting the Teachers' Association and without the consent of the latter.

Dr. _____ cited state law (citation) which permits any working conditions to be a matter of negotiations. He also stated that this is the practice in all districts with negotiated contracts. (85 percent of all districts in the state at this time.)

Mr. _____ cited state law (citation) which does not permit the board to delegate its power to make policy. He said that the proposed clause would delegate this power.

A discussion followed in which several speakers expressed opinions pro and con the argument that the clause under discussion constituted a violation of state law.

The superintendent reviewed the work of the policy council, citing the record of agreement on policies affecting working conditions. He stated that only one recommendation of the council was overruled by the board.

A discussion followed. Mrs. _____ pointed out that the one case cited by the superintendent proved the weakness of the council under present practices.

Dr. _____ asked if the board would approve a suitably worded insertion of teachers' rights to negotiate working conditions in the contract. The board agreed, provided the statement meets the legal restrictions previously cited.

AGREEMENT: A CLAUSE SHALL BE INSERTED IN THE CONTRACT ESTABLISHING THE RIGHT OF TEACHERS TO NEGOTIATE WORK-ING CONDITIONS. THE WORDING WILL BE DECIDED AT A FUTURE MEETING (DATE UN-SPECIFIED) AFTER EACH SIDE HAS PRE-PARED A PROPOSAL STATEMENT.

Further discussion followed on the legality of the clause as now written. The teachers' group refused to omit the word "con-sent." The board group refused further discussion unless the word is deleted.

The meeting was adjourned with no agreement as to the date, time, and place of the next meeting.

The undersigned agree that the foregoing minutes are ac-curate:

Recorder _____
Board Representative _____
Teachers' Representative _____

MEDIATION

Most states have laws providing for one or more stages of appeal in case of impasse. Mediation is not always binding on either party. Where no law spells out the procedure, both parties should agree on a procedure to be included in the first contract. The usual approach is a panel of three with one person selected by each party and the third member agreeable to the first two.

Where the law requires impasse mediation within a certain time limit, a letter is essential to verify that this has been done. A copy should be filed by the Superintendent and a copy should go to each chief negotiator. This is also recommended for any further correspon-dence on mediation.

Administrator to State Official:

Requesting mediation in negotiations

Dear _____:

The School Board and the teachers of _____ School District have reached an impasse in professional negotiations. According to Article _____ Bill _____ Ed. of the State

School Code, I am required to request the services of a mediator from the State Commissioner of Education.

I respectfully request your assistance in this matter at your earliest convenience. As soon as I have the name of your appointee I will proceed to make suitable arrangements for a meeting.

Respectfully,

Telephone contact should be made when the name arrives. Other letters will also be necessary. Top protocol is indicated for this VIP.

Administrator to Mediator:

Verifying details of meeting

Dear _____:

We are pleased that you have agreed to act as mediator in our negotiations impasse. As we agreed by telephone, the meeting will be held on October _____ at 7:30 P.M. in my office at _____ _____, _____.

I have reserved a room for you at the _____ Inn which is located next to the post office, on _____ in the center of _____.

Please call me at the office (_____) if you arrive before 5:30 P.M., or at my home (_____) after that time. I shall arrange for the other members of the team to meet you at the Inn. Let me know if you prefer to have dinner with them or to meet them after dinner. Coffee will be provided at the meeting place.

I have taken the liberty of enclosing some materials. Please call me (collect, person to person) if you wish any other materials or arrangements.

Enclosures
1. Salary schedules for the past five years.
2. Tax data for the past five years.
3. Statistics on student population, number of professional staff broken down by sex, degree status, experience, location on salary schedule.
4. Class size statistics.
5. Description of Policy Advisory Committee.
6. Photostats of minutes.
7. Copies of original proposals.
8. Expense form.

The District will reimburse your expenses. Please list them on the enclosed expense form and send this to me when you return home. I shall see that it receives prompt attention. Please do not hesitate to request anything you need to expedite your important task.

Sincerely,

Administrator to Mediator:

Thanking him for his services

Dear _____:

On behalf of the Board of Education of the _____ School District and myself, I wish to thank you for the fine professional services you performed in connection with our negotiations impasse. Having been deeply involved in the process which led to the impasse, I know how difficult your task was.

You may be certain that your recommendations will receive serious consideration by the Board and by me. Regardless of the positions now to be taken by both sides, your efforts will be certain to have a positive effect.

Gratefully,

Negotiations, as noted above, represent an area in which careless prose can cause vast harm. The case cited earlier (the failure to indicate in writing the length of the contract) did cause the district involved to endure a hectic year as Board and teachers insisted that the contract signed was for different periods of time. The chaos could have been avoided by the simple steps indicated in this chapter.

So, too, can all those other problems that arise when everyone trusts everyone else's memory of important details.

Get the agreements on paper. Get the details there too.

Anatomy of a Teacher Strike, by C. Vagts and R. Stone (West Nyack, N.Y.: Parker Publishing Co., Inc., 1969), may serve as a helpful aid in the question of communications dealing with teacher negotiations.

———◆———

ELEVEN

Your Own
Career Correspondence

For many years a struggle was waged in America to determine whether school administration was a function of a professional or that of a group of amateurs on a School Board. It was a rather one-sided battle for the most part. Only when it became painfully apparent that the amateurs had failed badly did they consent to let professionals handle the reins. Here and there the contest continues, but most American School Boards try to stick to policy making while their chief administrator makes the wheels turn.

A militant third force has emerged recently—the teachers' organization. Its moderate wing demands teacher participation in all matters affecting teachers' working conditions, including curriculum changes and policy formulation. Its extremist wing demands a virtual end to administration and the shift of decision making power to teachers' committees. Where the latter group wins substantial success, the superintendency will have risen from the manipulation of trivia into a position of consequence, only to revert back to its former low state of impotence.

However, the administrator has become more aggressive. This time he will not surrender without a fight. His calling has become a first class profession, albeit a cruelly demanding one, that is attempting to solve some of society's most difficult problems.

Recent years have seen tremendous changes in what the public expects of school administrators. School executives must quickly and thoroughly become familiar with the uses of automated data processing, with the best ways to use instructional television and other educational hardware. They must understand the advantages and limitations of scientific management systems. They must learn the skills of negotiations with militant employees' groups, professional and non-professional. They must be able to work patiently and fairly with angry minority groups and must understand the educational needs of seriously deprived children.

If you have done your homework in all of these areas, if you have prepared yourself professionally at the high level of current demands, if you have the patience of a saint along with the hide of a rhino and the persistence of an insurance salesman, opportunities can abound for you in educational administration.

Communications skills will be central prerequisites to your success in administration. Screening consultants, hiring authorities, and school boards are completely aware of this. They may not have an opportunity to hear you make a speech; in fact, your performance at an interview may be fairly brief. But they will have plenty of time to read and reread your letters of inquiry and application. These had better be good.

YOUR CAREER PLAN

Any career plan must begin with a fairly specific ultimate target. You may never reach it, but it must be there like a star to guide you on your way. Before you can choose a guiding star, however, you must ask yourself some tough questions and you must provide honest answers.

What do you want in a way of life? A city? A rural area? Suburbia? How important is a way of life when it collides with professional growth? How important will it become when you are older? Do you want to be a superintendent? If so, do you have a really good reason beyond the normal ambitions for power and money? How important will salary be to you when your children are grown and educated? These, and other questions, ranged in three basic steps, help prepare a career blueprint for you:

1. Get to know yourself well. You may need some objective, outside assistance with this.
2. Set a final goal for yourself that may be just beyond your grasp.

3. Move toward this goal in a logical and deliberate way, with no side trips for fun or for temporary convenience.

A decision to move ahead in administration should involve an *open* declaration. Too many teachers "protest too much" that they prefer to stay out of administration. Some of them are sincere, of course, but others secretly apply for administrative positions as soon as they appear. Denial of interest may be a form of insurance against loss of face, but secrecy is difficult to maintain in these matters and demonstrated hypocrisy is far more damning than failure to be chosen for advancement.

It is difficult to balance yourself between false humility and aggressive opportunism but it can be done. It must be done—especially in your career correspondence. Too much modesty in your interviews or in your correspondence may be interpreted as a sign of insecurity or, worse yet, deceit. Conversely, open boasting seldom creates a good impression.

PROMOTIONAL PAPERWORK

Besides the credentials you should have filed with the placement office of your university and, if you choose, with a commercial agency, you should always have on hand a current personal résumé. It should be as brief as possible but should contain all pertinent information. In addition to its uses in applying for better positions, it is a convenient document to send to the chairman of a function at which you have been asked to speak. At times it may be useful as a press handout.

There are many ways to organize a résumé. Here is one way which we have found effective:

FORMAT FOR A RÉSUMÉ

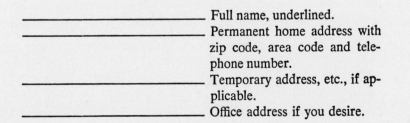

_____ Full name, underlined.
_____ Permanent home address with zip code, area code and telephone number.
_____ Temporary address, etc., if applicable.
_____ Office address if you desire.

PERSONAL DATA:

Date and place of birth, marital status, names and ages of children, date of marriage if you wish.

EDUCATION

Dates: Elementary and secondary schools attended. Locations. Public or private.

Dates: Undergraduate college. Name and location. Exact degree. Approximate semester hours in subject major and minor. The same information for professional courses. Where and when student teaching. Nature and extent of significant activities and sports.

Dates: Graduate study as above.

POSITIONS HELD

Outside of Education

Dates: In chronological order, describe the more significant (in terms of the time you spent on them) part-time and full-time jobs you have held. This may be of more than casual interest to the reader because it tells him something about you as a person.

In Education

Dates: Again, starting at the beginning, describe the exact positions you held along with the name, location, and size of the schools or districts. Describe your duties if any titles were vague, i.e. "administrative assistant." When your career involves two or more positions in one district, list the district as a major heading with each position as a subhead:

Bay City Unified School District, 1950–

1950–54 Teacher of English at West High School, JV Basketball Coach

1954–58 English Department Chairman at West High School, Varsity Basketball Coach

1958–62 Assistant Principal at East High School in charge of discipline and students activities

1962–65 Principal of East High School

1965–   Assistant District Superintendent for Personnel

PUBLICATIONS

List them unless they are extremely insignificant. Include names and dates of publications as well as titles of articles.

CONSULTANTSHIPS

List these chronologically and make clear the specific problem on which you worked. This would include participation in regional evaluation teams and service workshops.

ORGANIZATIONAL MEMBERSHIP

Here you list your civic and professional affiliations. You may wish to add your fellowships and scholarships, but take care that you do not compound trivia which is no substitute for a few major achievements.

If you have held administrative positions at the same level in two or more districts, be certain to indicate the number of pupils and teachers in the units of your responsibility.

You may want to list the top salaries earned in each position or location. Increases of salary and responsibility are the best explanation for moves. A move from a small principalship to an assistant principalship of a large school can be a promotion. Be certain that you indicate this or the move may be misunderstood.

LETTERS REQUESTING RECOMMENDATIONS

Whether or not you plan to move, you should periodically update your placement papers by having inserted current letters of reference from people familiar with your work, preferably (of course) from people who think well of you. Some placement offices require this if you wish to be considered for openings. Under normal conditions, there is no reason why you should hesitate to ask your superiors or your board members to do this. It is proper for school administrators to keep an eye on the job market.

You must have on file a letter of reference from your immediate superior. If he is unhappy with your work, you ought to have a plausible explanation of why he is wrong. Superintendents should turn to board members and, especially, to the board president for such letters. A superintendent can also seek credentials from the county superintendent (if there is one), and appropriate state officials. He should take care, however, that they indicate clearly that they have had a reasonable opportunity to evaluate his work. In some cases subordinates may be asked to write letters, but this is not usually worthwhile for obvious reasons.

A routine updating of references should be taken care of by requesting all letters of reference *at the same time*—if only to lend credence to the idea that it is routine. It is proper to indicate to the potential writers those matters which you would prefer to have stressed, such as heavy participation in planning new facilities.

If you merely wish to list a person as a possible reference without having him write a statement, you should still obtain permission. Thus, he will be prepared when a telephone call comes from a stranger asking for information about you. This is more delicate, however, for the call will indicate your active candidacy.

You can prevent needless calls by requesting in your applications that no checks be made with your references unless the employing district is considering your candidacy seriously. Most school administrators only check the references of top candidates, but occasionally eager beavers hold personnel positions and they demonstrate their efficiency by checking all references of everyone.

Administrator to Superior:

Requesting a reference

No such letter should go *to your immediate superior* since it is assumed you are in frequent personal contact. The proper way to handle this with your boss is face to face. No top administrator likes to learn suddenly that an immediate subordinate (especially an effective one) is a serious applicant for another position. In most cases a frank sharing of professional plans and aspirations is a part of the normal relationship at this level.

Dear Dr. _____ :

As you know, I am registered with the _____ University Placement Service. Each year the Placement Director asks that we upgrade our files regardless of immediate job interest.

I would be most grateful if you, as superintendent, would write a letter evaluating my work as assistant principal in _____ _____ High School. Normally, of course, superintendents in large districts like ours would not be in a position to offer a detailed evaluation of an assistant principal. I think my case is an exception since we did get to work together closely last year when _____ High was having its racial difficulties.

Mention of my handling of that problem would be appropriate in your letter since my immediate plans, *should I leave here,* would be for an urban principalship. Urban schools do tend to have whatever racial problems exist and the hiring of personnel in such districts would undoubtedly be interested in knowing that an applicant has had firing line experience.

A stamped addressed envelope is enclosed. Thank you for your help in this.

Sincerely,

CONTENT ANALYSIS

1. *The letter states clearly the reason for the requested letter of recommendation;*
2. *The letter indicates the writer's plans as plainly as possible;*
3. *The letter mentions a specific major achievement known to the potential letter writer and asks that some mention be made of that achievement.*

Administrator to Board Member:

Requesting a reference

Alternate 1 is for use when interested in a specific position.
Alternate 2 is for use in an updating of files.
Alternate 3 is for use when requesting a statement.

When interested in a specific position: Alternate 1

Dear Mr. _____ :

I would appreciate your permission to use your name as a reference in my candidacy for the position of Principal at _____ _____ High School in _____. This position would represent a significant upward move for me as well as a great professional challenge.

If you approve, you will probably be contacted by Dr. _____ _____, Superintendent of Schools at _____.

When updating files at Placement Service: Alternate 2

Dear Mr. _____ :

I would appreciate your permission to use your name as a reference in my efforts to move ahead to a principalship. As you know, I have been assistant principal here at _____ High

School for five years. I am not now an active candidate for a specific position, but I would like to be prepared if an opportunity for advancement presents itself.

Requesting a statement: Alternate 3

Dear Mr. _____:

I would appreciate your permission to use your name as a reference in a routine updating of my placement papers at _____ _____ University. I am not a candidate for any position at this time, but the Placement Office requires continued registration. I would be grateful for a statement from you on the enclosed form which should be sent directly to the University in the enclosed stamped, addressed envelope. The University maintains these references in strict confidence.

Closing Statement for all these alternatives

This request does not reflect any dissatisfaction on my part with my present position or with any person in this district. In our profession we have a relatively short period of time to take advantage of opportunities to move ahead. We must be prepared to do so or opportunity will pass us by.

I feel that you are familiar with my work, especially (insert here some achievement with which the addressee is familiar). I also feel that you understand the difficult choices which sometimes must be made by administrators. I would appreciate your keeping this matter in confidence to prevent any misunderstanding. I have informed (the name of your immediate superior) of my plans and of this request.

Respectfully,

Superintendent to Board Member:

Requesting a reference

Dear _____:

As you know, a superintendent's job is a difficult one. Recently it has become a rapidly changing one. A successful man can, in the midst of this change, become suddenly a failure.

I believe that the Superintendency is too important to too many people for anyone holding it to lean on tenure for security.

The top man must rely on his continued effective judgment and action for his continuation in the position.

Most of us try to maintain current placement papers as a reasonable avenue of security. My papers are filed with the Placement Office of the Graduate School of Education at _____ _____ University. Since they require bi-annual updating, I would appreciate very much a statement from you on the enclosed placement form. If you are willing, it should be mailed in the enclosed stamped, addressed envelope directly to the placement office where it will be confidentially filed.

I feel that you were satisfied with my leadership in the recent busing crisis. It would be to my advantage if you made a reference to this.

I assure you that this request does not represent any dissatisfaction on my part with the cooperation of the present Board of Education or with any part of my work here. It is merely a routine action which must be done periodically by anyone.

The closing salutation, omitted here, would depend upon the specific relationship of this superintendent with this Board member.

Requests sent to fellow professionals do not require the explanation at the beginning of the letter. These should, however, contain references to important achievements of yours with which the potential writers are familiar. For maximum effect you should spread your achievements among several people.

All letters of this type should include a stamped envelope, addressed to the appropriate placement offices.

ABOUT PRIVATE AGENCIES

Unless you have limited access to a university placement office, or unless your university does a poor job in placement, it is probably wiser not to request these statements for private agencies. If you do, many will consider that (1) your university placement office does not consider you a good candidate or (2) that you are extremely anxious to move. This is especially true if it becomes known that you are registered in several agencies. This is a case where the real truth is less important than what people think is true.

There is nothing intrinsically wrong with using a private agency if you are ready to pay the fee, which is 5 percent or more of your entering annual salary. For a superintendent obtaining a $25,000 position this is quite a blow, even if it is deductible on his income tax. However, many private agencies do a fine job—much better than some college agencies. *In some cases* it is possible to register with a private agency without soliciting statements of reference provided that you and the agency understand that you will request your university to forward your papers to the lead obtained from the private agency. This process, however, skirts the edge of ethical behavior.

It is best to choose one private agency carefully if you decide to use this method. A personal interview with an officer of the agency can be of great benefit to both of you. No agency, public or private, can represent you optimally in placement unless it knows you as a human being rather than merely as a pile of papers.

LETTERS OF INQUIRY

In recent years school boards have begun to turn to consultants for help in finding candidates for top positions, especially superintendents. These consultants are usually professors (active or emeritus) of educational administration. It is not always good form to contact them about a specific position. They are supposed to find you.

If, on the other hand, you hear of a vacancy in a district which appeals to you for some good reason, it is appropriate to write directly to the School Board. *Be certain, before you do, that the vacancy actually exists.*

In a case like this, the following guidelines should be observed:

1. Include a résumé with your letter.
2. Indicate why you are particularly interested in *this* position.
3. Indicate that you know something about the specific problems of the District. (Find out what they are. Use your ingenuity.)
4. Indicate why you are specifically prepared to solve these problems.
5. Indicate where they may obtain your placement folder.
6. Indicate your availability for interview.
7. Request confidential handling of the matter, if you desire, until you are considered, by them, to be a prime candidate.
8. Make it clear that this is a letter of inquiry and not a formal application.
9. In the case of a superintendency, find out the name of the Chair-

man or President of the Board and address the letter to him personally. It is best to determine the correct title—whether this is a school committee, a School Board, a Board of School Directors, or whatever.

10. In the case of a position below the superintendency, direct the inquiry to the superintendent by name.

Superintendent to Board President:

Inquiring about a position

Dear Mr. _____:

I have been informed that you are seeking candidates for the Superintendency of the _____ School District. I am not actively seeking a change at this time. However, I am making this preliminary inquiry because your District interests me for a number of reasons.

I have followed your excellent building program with particular interest. Your plan for the creation of a central middle school is quite sound. As the enclosed résumé indicates, I have had considerable experience with plant planning and construction and I have participated in the creation of a middle school.

_____ represents the type of community in which I would like to raise my youngest son. It would give him an opportunity to become familiar with all facets of American life rather than with only a protected suburb.

Since this is a letter of inquiry, I would appreciate the matter being held in confidence at this stage.

I would welcome an opportunity to discuss this with you and the Board. My credentials may be obtained at your request from the Placement Office of the Graduate School of Education at _____ University.

My home address is _____.

My telephone number is _____.

Sincerely,

Letters of inquiry to a placement office can be more direct but they should indicate some deference to the screening function carried out by the placement officials. Use the name of the official handling your type of position. A telephone call is indicated if you are uncertain about this.

Administrator to a College Placement Office:

Inquiry about a specific position

Dear Dr. _____:

  Although I am not actively seeking a change at this time, I am interested for many reasons in the Superintendency at _____ _____. If you consider me a suitable candidate, I would like to request your support in the matter. I have written a preliminary letter of inquiry to the President of the Board.

                Respectfully,

  This could, of course, put the placement office on the spot. They may have several people they consider more suitable for the position. If you are concerned that the placement officer will discriminate against you in the future, you should make the inquiry to him *before* you write to the Board President. If you really want the job, however, you must proceed directly and honestly as above. The worst that will probably happen is that a covering letter will accompany your credentials making it clear that they are sent at *your* request and do not have the endorsement of the placement office.

  Few placement officials discriminate because of minor annoyance. Most try to fit the candidates to the positions. Candidates for top administrative positions should become personally acquainted with the placement officer handling this category. The simplest way to do this is to make an appointment for a frank chat with him.

LETTERS OF APPLICATION

  A letter of application need not be lengthy. It is merely a formal notice that your hat is firmly and officially in the ring. It should be sent as soon as you have made your decision, and may consist of only one sentence. It helps the screening group if you make reference to previous steps which you might have taken. They will probably be handling many applications and papers can be misplaced when they pass through many hands. A letter of application should be sent to the person assigned by the hiring authority to handle correspondence. If no such person is indicated, it should be addressed to the superintendent if it concerns a lower position than his, to the President of the Board if it concerns the superintendency.

Administrator to Board:

Formal application for a position

Dear Miss ——————:

I wish to submit my candidacy for the Superintendency of the ————————— School District.

I sent a letter of inquiry and a résumé to Mr. ————————— on April 24th. I received your brochure shortly thereafter and had a preliminary discussion with the Board on April 30th. Mr. ————————— indicated that he had received my placement folder from ————————— University on April 29th.

If there is any further material desired by the Board, please let me know.

Yours very truly,

This letter provides a handy reference for the Board. Now they can review your folder and check the materials against this letter. At least one Board member (the secretary) will be happy with your candidacy: You will have shown thoughtfulness about her task. Now all you have to do is convince the rest of the Board that you are the man for the job.

Do not try to "snow them under" with a great deal of supportive evidence such as testimonial letters, newspaper clippings, etc. Some of this is justified and desirable. If you have a *good* brochure for teacher recruitment or a printed budget message that you can be proud of, send enough copies for each Board member. They are always interested in public relations materials. But don't overdo it.

APPLICATION FORMS

Many districts require that each candidate for an administrative post fill out their lengthy teacher application form, thereby duplicating most of the material in your placement folder. The usual reason for this is that the decision makers are familiar with their form and they can quickly find on it a given item. It also makes it easier for them to complete a preliminary screening of candidates who are lacking one or more of the published requirements for the job.

Fill out these application forms carefully and legibly (type them

if possible), even though much of the material may have no bearing
on the position you are seeking. If, for example, the question appears,
"Do you play the piano?", answer it. Perhaps they want you to play
for group singing at a School Board convention. Who knows?

LETTERS OF RESIGNATION

It never pays to burn too many bridges behind you no matter
how much you disliked the position you are leaving. Always be fair
and ethical with your employer in giving him a reasonable opportunity to replace you—at least with an acting appointee. Always offer
to spend some time (if at all possible) with the person replacing you
to answer any questions he may have. Leave your office in good order
and free of your personal bric-a-brac. If you wish to take with you any
materials you helped to develop, such as a policy book, request it
formally of the proper authority. Above all, do not make any brash
statements which you would not have made before you received your
new contract elsewhere.

Address your letter of resignation to the Superintendent if you
hold lesser rank, or to the President of the Board if you are a Superintendent.

Superintendent to Board:

Letter of resignation.

Dear Mr. _____ :

It is with regret that I resign my position as Superintendent
of Schools in the _____ School District.

I have enjoyed the challenges of the position but my concern for my career growth and for my family make it necessary
to accept a new position with greater responsibilities in a larger
district. (Name the job if you care to.)

I shall always be grateful for the cooperation of the Board
and of the staff. I am particularly indebted to my secretary, Miss
_____ , for outstanding devotion to her work, and to the
wisdom and untiring efforts of Dr. _____ , my Deputy, in
his service to the students of our District.

I would like to assume my new duties by July 1. However,
I shall be available until you find a suitable replacement for me

and until he has had an opportunity to question me if he should choose to do so. Please let me know your desires in this matter.

Respectfully,

In conclusion, we think that the school administrator, a man who earns his living by his ability to communicate, owes it to himself to display this ability when carrying out that correspondence which directly concerns his job. Now, more than at any other time, a man puts his reputation in the open for all to see. Thus, now is the time when extreme prudence should be exercised.

A FINAL WORD

We have offered much advice and many samples in the preceding pages. Like most authors, we would like to sum it all up in a pithy sentence or two or a universal time-saver. We think, though, that this would be misleading. No writing is ever really easy, especially not the writing of a good letter. We do not want, in any way, to imply that anything less than real effort is sufficient in letter writing.

That, then, is our final advice: Work at your letter writing, polish your efforts, rewrite them, follow all the rules we offered earlier in this book, and, when all else is done, remember what Winston Churchill advised:

Short words are better than long words
And old words are best of all.

PART A

Letters Index

The Index is divided into two parts.

Part A contains a listing of all the letters and memos which appear in the book. These are arranged according to the title of the person sending the letter. Thus, as an example, the letter sent to an applicant to indicate that his application has been received appears under the heading ADMINISTRATOR TO . . .

Part B of the Index contains a subject listing of topics or items which are of more than usual interest to the reader. No letters are listed in this section of the Index.

PART B

Subject Index